THE STORY OF **YOU**

The Story of You demonstrates the power we all have to take control of our lives no matter what our pasts look like. Mark combines his personal story with extraordinary leadership lessons (and the stick-figure art skills of an above-average kindergartener) to give hope and practical wisdom to help you take control of your future.

—**Nick Pavlidis**, Vice President /
Chief Terrible Husband
at ATerribleHusband.com

The Story of You will wake up the dreams, passions, and visions you had as a child. Read it and grab this new opportunity to make your own dream shine!

—**Dan Miller**, New York Times bestselling author
48 Days to the Work You Love

Minard learned that powerful things happen when you read books and even more powerful things happen when you apply them. He tells the story of discovering and doing his life's work and shows you how to do the same, even if you're stuck in a Weiner Dog Drive Thru at 2 am - literally or figuratively.

—**Emily Chase Smith**, Writing Partner,
www.ChaseSmithPress.com,
Phone (949) 391-6063

THE STORY OF
YOU

TRANSFORMING ADVERSITY INTO ADVENTURE,
TAKING YOUR DREAMS TO THE NEXT LEVEL AND
→**BEYOND**←

MARK MINARD

New York

THE STORY OF **YOU**
TRANSFORMING ADVERSITY INTO ADVENTURE,
TAKING YOUR DREAMS TO THE NEXT LEVEL AND BEYOND

Published in New York, New York, by Morgan James Publishing. Morgan James and The Entrepreneurial Publisher are trademarks of Morgan James, LLC.
www.MorganJamesPublishing.com

The Morgan James Speakers Group can bring authors to your live event. For more information or to book an event visit The Morgan James Speakers Group at
www.TheMorganJamesSpeakersGroup.com.

Shelfie

A **free** eBook edition is available
with the purchase of this print book.

CLEARLY PRINT YOUR NAME ABOVE IN UPPER CASE

Instructions to claim your free eBook edition:
1. Download the Shelfie app for Android or iOS
2. Write your name in **UPPER CASE** above
3. Use the Shelfie app to submit a photo
4. Download your eBook to any device

ISBN 978-1-63047-789-9 paperback
ISBN 978-1-63047-791-2 eBook
ISBN 978-1-63047-792-9 audio
ISBN 978-1-63047-790-5 hardcover
Library of Congress Control Number:
2015914976

Edited by:
Fate Publishing

Cover Design by:
Chris Treccani
www.3dogdesign.net

Interior Design by:
Bonnie Bushman
The Whole Caboodle Graphic Design

In an effort to support local communities and raise awareness and funds, Morgan James Publishing donates a percentage of all book sales for the life of each book to Habitat for Humanity Peninsula and Greater Williamsburg.

Get involved today, visit
www.MorganJamesBuilds.com

Habitat
for Humanity®
Peninsula and
Greater Williamsburg
Building Partner

I dedicate this to my wife, Iyeba Minard, as she is my partner in our very own Story of You, through thick and through thin, and I'm incredibly grateful.

TABLE OF CONTENTS

FOREWORD

When I was just 13 years old my life was dramatically impacted by a little recording called *The Strangest Secret*. The message presented was essentially the Biblical principle – "As a man thinketh in his heart, so is he," but it resonated with me as a clear path to expand my opportunities. I learned the power of feeding my mind positive, faith-building thoughts as opposed to allowing the challenges of a legalistic religion and a poor farm life to determine my attitude and future. And I learned that by taking responsibility for my thinking I could determine the direction of my life. I discovered we can all choose to tell our life story as a victim or as one who has chosen to walk in victory and abundance.

In this very hopeful book Mark shares his own story of early heartache, tragedy and bad decisions – and how those experiences could have left him trapped in anger, fear and mediocrity. But his continued search for answers and solutions also led to his discovery that he was not trapped – he had a choice. He could move beyond those negative emotions and actions to live out a big WHY.

Mark also discovered the power of filling his mind with positive, faith-building thoughts. Choosing to read great books of the ages opened the door to the truths by which he has formed his own principles of success:

- It's okay to be terrible on the way to being great.
- At the root of indecision is fear.
- Like Linus in the Peanuts comic strip, most of us feel afraid, apprehensive or unsure and that can stop us or direct us.
- Once we get comfortable we tend to stay that way as long as we can. It takes clear action to move into new opportunities.
- A big dream creates a big WHY
- We all have disadvantages - some are perhaps more obvious to others while some we can hide pretty well.
- Failure is just one of those necessary steps on the way to success.
- Keep taking action or you could end up in "the land of mediocrity."
- When you have nothing, anything is possible.
- We must move from knowledge to understanding, to application.

We all dream of and wish for lives of happiness, meaning and fulfillment. And yet, it seems that reality assures us that we will experience hardships along the way. God has apparently designed us to grow from the unexpected struggles that inevitably show up. But like the butterfly struggling to get out of the cocoon, our struggles are part of what makes us fully alive. And like the butterfly, those struggles are not intended to limit or cripple us, but to allow us to develop our resilience, fortitude, compassion and personal excellence.

In *The Story of You*, Mark shares his own remarkable story of building Dreamshine, a place where adults with special needs can spend their days in a supportive and productive environment. Where others may see hopelessness and resignation, Mark see opportunities for enriching activities that include vocational training and generous compensation for work completed. In addition there is plenty of time for swimming, gardening, dancing and fishing.

Even the name Dreamshine evokes the desire we all have to live out our unique passions and childhood dreams. And this book provides more than just looking in at someone else's dream. You'll be given a roadmap for the fulfillment of your own.

You will be guided to understand your "why" as the starting point for "what do you want to do." The more you know yourself, the more confidence you can have about creating a life that fits you. And the more you know about yourself, the more you recognize the freedom you have in choosing work that is meaningful, purposeful, and profitable. It doesn't matter if you are eighteen or sixty eight - this process can work for you. For many of you, *The Story of You* will present a process of waking up the dreams, passions, and visions you had as a child. For some of you the mergers, downsizings, firings, forced retirements and other forms of unexpected change in the workplace in the last few years have served as a clarion wake-up call for dreams that have been waiting patiently for rebirth. Maybe you have been given the opportunity to take a fresh look at "Who am I and why am I here?"

Immerse yourself in this book, allow a fresh expression of those deep urgings that you may have been repressing in your desire to be responsible and mature. The moment you realize that meaningful, purposeful, and profitable work really is a possibility, you've already taken an important step toward reawakening the dreams and passions you may have waiting for release and expression. All of a sudden, complacency and "comfortable misery" become intolerable. The idea of putting your dream on the shelf becomes unacceptable.

I challenge you to open your heart and discover how the unexplained and often unwelcomed events in our lives can move us toward the greatness intended for each of us. As we move away from our own hurts and fears, we release the best in ourselves and encourage the same in those around us. Not only do you have the opportunity, you have the responsibility to find or create work that will elevate you to your highest calling - Let your dream shine!

—**Dan Miller**, New York Times bestselling author of
48 Days to the Work You Love

PREFACE

Why stick figures in a leadership book, you ask?! Why not! You see, *The Story of You* all began with this stick drawing, "The Grass is Greener on the Other Side," drawn by me in August of 2014. This little stick-figure drawing then sparked a new area of my creativity in which I had a vision of writing a book about my story of overcoming adversity, discovering my passion, my Faith, my dreams, and sharing my real-life stories from in the trenches of HOW I did all this, and HOW you can too! I realized I had read over 85 books in the past year-and-a-half on leadership and personal development and although I had read some amazing ones, a lot of them began to look like the same blah, blah, blah... So, rather than complaining about it, I decided that I'm going to share my own story and throw in my own stick figure illustrations throughout the book to add in a little flavor. So, as you read *The Story of You*, you will find my original stick-figure drawings (you can even see eraser mark and maybe even a misspelled word or two, haha). Because *The Story of*

You is all about the authentic....YOU! Eraser marks, misspelled words, and all. "Stick drawings in a leadership, personal development book, Mark, that's IMPOSSIBLE!" you declare. And I so wonderfully reply, "Impossible is where every great adventure begins." Which brings us here together, as we embark on the story of you.

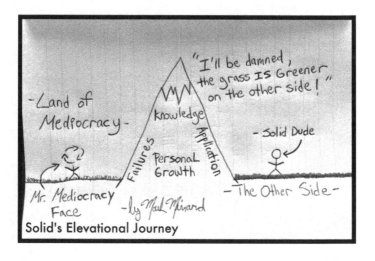

Solid's Elevational Journey

BROKEN BONES, JAIL, AND PET SEMATARY

"Success is the ability to go from one failure to the other with no loss of enthusiasm."
—Winston Churchill

Reading changed my life.

It pulled me up and out of a dark place where there were parties, drugs, alcohol, broken bones, and jail when I was 17 years old. It took the adversity of getting my face smashed in by a 35-year-old cowboy dude who I rear-ended in a Weiner Dog Drive Thru at 2.a.m. I was so intoxicated, I was like a catatonic punching bag. This very angry dude broke my jaw and fractured the bone under my left eye socket. I don't remember any of it. I just remember waking up on the cold, hard jail cell floor. As the police officer took my mug shots, he told me what happened. He also told me that my blood alcohol level was so high that I should have died. This was the worst and the best thing that ever happened to me.

Sometimes we all need a beautiful backhand of perspective.

The trouble I was in because of my behavior and the choices I was making paralyzed me. It made me less than the person I could be. I doubted myself and was going nowhere. And then I read a book.

It was something I had never done before. Throughout high school, when my teachers assigned books to read, I never read them. Not a whole book, anyways. But here I was, broken, beaten, and at the bottom of my game. I picked up a copy of *Pet Sematary*, a horror novel written by Stephen King in 1983, and for the first time in my life, I read an entire book.

Me.

I was so excited about reading. I remember going to sleep reading that book and waking up in the morning to read. I became lost in Stephen King's words and descriptions. It wasn't a book about how to change my life, but this book did just that. It expanded my mind and changed me forever. That one, first book that I read from cover to cover years ago ignited a passion in me for reading. And as a result, I discovered who I was meant to be.

Before reading *Pet Sematary* I may have doubted myself, but I never doubted my God. For as long as I can remember, I have always known God and had a relationship with him. I accepted Jesus into my heart and prayer became an important part of my life. Even through the partying, the troubles, and the poor decision-making, I knew God still loved me. I continued to pray and talk to him. But at the same time, I knew I wasn't being everything he wanted me to be. And as a result, I wasn't seeing God's fruits in my life because of the choices I was making and the way I was living.

I have heard it said many times that knowledge is power. But that's not exactly true. I believe knowledge applied is what truly equals power.

You can read 1,000 books, all of which will elevate your mindset, but unless you apply what you've read, it is all sadly wasted. I learned this first hand. As I read my way through Stephen King's words, the descriptions of the setting and events in the story changed my mindset, or my ideas and attitudes. From there I read more fiction, science fiction, and novels of all kinds. I was reading and reading and expanding my mind. The year I started reading, I went from never having read a book, to reading 26 books. Then I discovered reading with a purpose. Just this past year, I have read 65 books on leadership. I chose to do that because I wanted to develop my skills to the next level. I wanted to be the best leader I could be, so I immersed myself in reading.

The more knowledge you have, the more wisdom you have.

It doesn't stop there, however. Knowledge and wisdom needs to be applied. Once applied, all of that knowledge and wisdom becomes power. From there, that power can be used in different ways. For me, having the power means having more ability to serve other people. Helping people creates a ripple effect of greatness. And this means spreading God's word. Spreading God's kingdom is power. Last year, when I read dozens of books about leadership, I read them in the spirit of application. In order to build my team management skills, I used information from the experts who wrote all of those books and then walked their walk.

Application is everything.

Application is power.

Reading that first book all the way through to the end changed my life. This book you are holding in your hands has the potential to do the same for you. It can get you thinking about things from a different perspective. It can get you excited about something that will help you in your own life. And it can change your life.

Welcome to my story. I hope my journey can help you with yours.

BEING BRAVE

"I learned that courage is not the absence of fear, but the triumph over it. The brave man is not he who does not feel afraid, but he who conquers that fear."
—Nelson Mandela

O ne of the pivotal changes in my life was when I started reading. I cannot say enough about how that has changed my life. So I will say it again: Reading alone has changed my life. But once something has moved you to change something within yourself, you become hungry to continue growing. As you continue to grow, there will be more pivotal moments. Mine came next while I was in college.

I started attending Colorado State University in 1998. I looked like every other student there. I was pretty social, had a lot friends, and attended classes like everyone else. Inside, however, I was plagued with voices of doubt and panic. These feelings increased and became overwhelming. It got to the point where I was enveloped by anxiety and felt like I was having a heart attack. My heart would pound in my chest with no warning, rhyme or reason. Beads of sweat would pour down my face. Drenched in sweat and feeling like I was going to fall to the ground and have a full-blown heart attack, I was forced to abruptly leave class. I would run to the bathroom and splash water on my face.

"What is happening to me?" I'd say to the terrified face in the mirror. "Lord, please make this stop."

After this happened a few times, the anticipation of having another anxiety attack would cause me to be afraid. I was embarrassed and terrified. The fear of something that might or might not happen set me up to have another one.

According to the Anxiety and Depression Association of America's website, a panic attack is the abrupt onset of intense fear or discomfort that reaches a peak within minutes and includes at least four of the following symptoms: pounding heart; sweating, trembling or shaking; feeling short of breath; feelings of choking; chest pain; nausea; dizziness; chills; numbness or tingling; feelings of detachment or unreality; fear of going crazy; or fear of dying.[1] I felt alone, but discovered that anxiety disorders are "one of the most common mental health problems on college campuses."[2] In fact, mental health conditions have been found to begin during the typical college age range of 18 to 24 years. The National Institute of Mental Health says that 75 percent of all people who are challenged with an anxiety disorder will experience their first symptoms while they are in college.

I was one of them.

In her article about college students and mental health, Margarita Tartakovsky, M.S., attributes the significant life transition that young people experience when they go off to college as a factor. She goes on to say that dealing with so many firsts – a new way of life, new friends, having a roommate, and learning to think in a different way – can make some young adults feel ill-prepared. This leads to a lack of confidence which shakes what they know about their own identities. Loss of sense of who we are, says Tartakovsky, can lead to depression and anxiety.[3]

The more I read about anxiety and depression, the more I learned about what I was experiencing and what I could do about it. This goes back to applying what you read. I read and practiced deep breathing exercises to settle my heart rate and increase the oxygen in my blood. I knew this was something I had to deal with and it then became another defining moment in my life. I had to find a way to not allow the panic attacks I was experiencing to stop me from going to classes. I turned to scripture. In Isaiah 54:7, I read "no weapon formed against me shall prosper." I had to find a way to not allow the panic attacks to stop me from going to classes. I had to be brave. I had to keep going and reading, praying, deep breathing and ultimately, graduate from college.

And I did!

In looking back, I realized that part of my anxiety was due to introspection, my own self-awareness issues and how I thought about myself. In college, I tended to overanalyze what I said to people and what they thought about what I said to them. I would overanalyze to the point that my anxiety level would elevate and cause panic attacks. Then I would wonder if people thought I was crazy when my face randomly turned red and gushed massive beads of sweat. In general, I don't think it's bad to overanalyze, but when it becomes an obsession, that's when it can do some real harm. I even dropped speech class three times in college, terrified I'd have an anxiety attack while giving a speech.

I work on this still. Even though it's been years, I work at being conscious and aware of my thoughts. If I am quiet and think about something all day, I am procrastinating. Procrastination makes me anxious. Anxiety makes me fearful. After more procrastination - because now I am anxious and fearful and nothing is getting done - I worry. Then I worry about the worry. Ultimately, nothing gets done at all. Procrastination is a form of paralysis. I am not only wasting my time, I am wasting the actions I could be taking. Now when this happens - when I find myself obsessing over something I said - I take action. I counteract those invasive thoughts that in the past have led to feelings of anxiety and panic. I do this by thinking about the now.

Biblically, the whole idea about worrying leads nowhere. In Matthew 6:27, God says, "Can any one of you by worrying add a single hour to your life?" In other words, worrying accomplishes absolutely nothing. Proverbs 12:25a says, "Anxiety weighs down the heart," which tells us that worrying is not good for us. Worrying also takes our focus off God and the things he wants us to do. In Matthew 5:34, God says, "Therefore do not worry about tomorrow, for tomorrow will worry about itself. Each day has enough trouble of its own."[4] When I read these verses, I understand just how time-consuming and useless worrying can be. So bottom line is when you are feeling overwhelmed and obsessed with thoughts of self-doubt and what others think of you, just start thinking about the now.

When I learned to focus on the moment at hand, I saw myself accomplish more. And as I am accomplishing more and more with my life, I am learning to manage my time better. By not procrastinating, I find myself getting much more done. It's not that I am less busy – I own a company, I have five children, and am writing my first book (Thanks for buying it.) – it's that I have learned to start doing things at this moment in time. Right now. One of the many things I've read about truly successful people is that they are intentional about the way they spend their time. Learning to manage my time and not procrastinate is an ongoing battle for me. No one is ever perfect at that. But we can all get better at it. With hard work, I can say that I am in charge of my own time.

Are you in charge of your time?

Something I do that helps me make time for my family and busy work days and everything else I want and need to do is to schedule times in my calendar. I block out time and am intentional and specific about how I do it. Let's go back to the question I just asked you: Are you in charge of your time? Spend a few minutes right now and think about that. Jot down areas of your life that you feel are not getting your full attention. The attention God wants you to give. Maybe it's spending time with your children. Maybe it's going out on a date with your spouse. Whatever it is, all things are possible if you are intentional and work as hard as you can to not procrastinate.

What's so great about getting what you need to get done? For me, it is seeing the fruits that God has promised me. It is being able to love and spend time with my wife and children and family members. It is being able to run an incredible business staffed by caring and professional people. It helped me stay on course as I navigated the system to start my business. And with hundreds of different things that could have stopped my dreams before they even became a reality, my passion for helping people and strength of character won out. But before I tell you how it all began, I want to tell you about Dreamshine.

WHERE ALL PEOPLE SHINE

⟶ ⟵ ⟶ ⟵

"We are so grateful for the high quality programming and the caring all of you show on a daily basis to our daughter. She is very happy at Dreamshine and she has grown as a result of being in your program. Thank you again for all you and your staff do."
—**Rebecca**, mother

A t Dreamshine, everyone can fish. We've built a one-level, fully wheelchair accessible waterfront lodge that overhangs a sparkling pond stocked with fish. But fishing is not the only thing that sets our program apart. It is a place where adults with special needs can spend their days productively in a supportive and nurturing environment. People who come to Dreamshine can earn paychecks, volunteer and participate in community organizations, and strengthen their educational and social skills. Each day is filled with therapeutic recreation, gardening, dancing, and exploration. At Dreamshine, each individual is treated with respect, dignity, and given the chance to shine.

And this is my why. But before I talk about what a why is, I want you to really understand what it is that I do. This way you can see how much the why matters when you are trying to build something that will make a difference.

Dreamshine is an adult day program that provides education in life skills, social skills, and healthy living skills to men and women with special needs. Our mission is to ensure the highest quality of independence, personal growth, and social interaction. To do this, we provide a safe and caring environment where our participants have opportunities to explore new interests and activities while having fun. Because we are an innovative program, people who attend have the chance to pursue their own individual interests. And how each person spends his or her day here at Dreamshine is tailored to those individual interests and his or her individual needs.

In addition to our fully stocked pond, we have a hot tub, adaptive gardens, fruit trees, a log home and waterfront lodge with breathtaking views, rabbits, an outdoor cat, fish, and a lovebird for animal therapy. Our full-sized hot tub provides a beautiful view of the woods, pine trees and pond, making it feel like you are at a resort in the mountains. My staff and I care about our friends who attend our program and make sure they have every opportunity they seek available to them. For example, we have volunteer opportunities at *My Very Own Blanket*, an organization which provides personalized blankets and other items to children in foster care, *Helpline of Delaware*, a local, toll-free crisis support, information and referral hotline for people living in Delaware and Morrow counties, Ohio, and *Forgotten No More, Inc.*, an organization that trains and supports people with intellectual challenges – people who have been deserted and forgotten by society. This program is part of my sister, Amy Minard's adventure, the Grace Center Ethopia. Based in Ethiopia, the staff supports participants with programs for life and social skills and vocational and educational skills. They work to prepare these individuals for life in society, and to prepare and bring awareness to society, as well.

We do the same here in Ohio.

Not only can the men and women who attend Dreamshine learn new skills, but they can continue their education, too. Educational assessments are conducted and lesson plans created to benefit the goals and aspirations of each individual desiring to further themselves academically. We also offer a wide range of vocational and recreational opportunities. And these are tailored to fit the needs of each Dreamshine participant. For example, there is bowling, coffee outings, trips to the library, swimming, massage therapy, educational tutoring, daily exercise sessions, social skills groups, and ballroom dancing. Everyone here has a choice and the opportunity to learn to make handmade, quality items from scratch, learn to garden, care for pets, and learn the value of team work.

As people work, they earn above-minimum wages and see the benefits of their work. That's because the items created at Dreamshine, which include hand poured Buckeye gourmet chocolates, apple pie, hand poured soy wax candles, comfort crosses, and more, including special holiday items, are sold in our online stores with 100 percent of the profits going back into activities and special programming chosen by our participants.

We have a store in Sunbury, Ohio, and we also ship our products anywhere in the United States. (If you are interested in seeing what we have, go to our website at http://www.dreamshine.co/dreamshine_country_store and check us out.)

Dreamshine is my life. It's my passion. It's my why. It's what I get up and do every day. Being at Dreamshine and working with my accomplished staff and our awesome participants makes all the sleepless nights, funding issues, rules and regulations, and hard work pay off.

There were hundreds of different things that have happened along the way that I could have justified just giving up. Even people who I was close to told me it would be too hard, too much and I should give up. But I knew deep down that my passion to help these men and women with special needs was much stronger than the obstacles I would face. I fought one battle at a time, and after all of that, I have all of this to show for it.

And now, at Dreamshine, everyone can fish.

THE JOURNEY BEGINS

→ ← → ←

B efore Dreamshine, before I realized my why, I graduated from college and moved from Colorado to Ohio to work with my brother in his tile business. I held a B.S. in Psychology with a focus on brain physiology and was planning to go on to graduate school to work toward my doctorate in child psychology. But, I decided I wanted a break from college, so working with my older brother, Chip, was perfect. My parents raised me to always embrace the value of working hard, and I had been working different jobs since I was 15 ½ years old. My first job, actually, was at Taco Bell. I had spent the last summer doing labor for my brother and his tile company. I always valued the importance of working hard. Soon after I arrived, however, I was given the opportunity to work with adults with special needs.

I was hired to work at The Workshop, a county-run day program for adults with mental and physical challenges. According to the U.S. Department of Health and Human Services, an adult day program in Ohio is currently defined as "a nonresidential community-based

13

service designed to meet the needs of functionally and/or cognitively impaired adults through an individualized care plan that encourages optimal capacity for self-care and/or maximizes functional abilities. It consists of structured, comprehensive, and continually supervised components that are provided in a protective setting."[5] The definition goes on to describe two levels of care: enhanced adult services, which includes the supervision of all daily living activities. Care workers for enhanced adult day services administer medications and provide hands-on assistance with one daily living task (except bathing), supervise comprehensive therapeutic activities, and assess and monitor the health of clients and options to participate in community activities. The second level is intensive adult day service. Here, clients receive all services in the enhanced program, as well as help with two or more daily living activities, such as bathing, nursing assistance, rehabilitation, physical therapy, speech therapy, occupational therapy, and social work services.

When I began working with special needs adults in the early 2000s, families had two choices: They could either have their family member stay at home all day doing nothing, or send them to county-run workshops. Families that chose to send their sons or daughters to these places knew they were safe and kept busy. And while they weren't abused or treated poorly, the only two options at these very large, very institutional-looking places were to put machine parts together or color. And both activities were with little interaction with others.

I found this to be very sad.

My niece had been diagnosed with autistic tendencies and the thought of her spending her days at these giant warehouses with awful fluorescent lights either working or coloring was so disheartening to me. This was all there was for her after she would graduate from her special education program in high school. And it broke my heart. I worked there for about four months and then got a job managing a group home. I loved working with special needs adults and here I had the chance to see how things really worked in the home environment. As a manager, I saw firsthand the different ways things were done on good levels and on not-so-good levels. It was cool, and yet discouraging at the same time. Some areas of care needed so much more. I saw how poor leadership at the upper levels destroyed the unity on every level and created a very mediocre culture. I am not one to talk badly of the place that pays my salary – I made the choice to work there and had the option to leave – however, I did make mental notes of what not to do. I learned to be intentional to avoid creating a mediocre culture. This fueled my passion to want to make a way to create better services on every level for people with special needs.

That's when I decided to start learning all I could about leadership. I was already gaining experience in managing different teams and working with all kinds of people, but I knew I needed more if I wanted to make a change. Not too long after, I got a job offer to work in a special education program in Columbus. For two years, I worked with special needs high school students in two classrooms. This was a great job for me. Not only did I love what I was doing, but it gave me insight into what would happen to these wonderful students after they graduated. And this brought me back to square one: These young adults would either be sitting at home all day doing nothing, or attending the county program where they would not be getting the social, educational, and vocational skills they needed and deserved. I knew that for two out of the 24 students I had worked with, this was an appropriate fit. But for the other 22 young people, this was unacceptable, and no one was doing anything about it.

I believe that we, as human beings, have options. We get to choose whether we finish high school, or not. We get to choose to go on to college, or not. We get to choose where we want to apply and work. But for these individuals, there were no choices. It was the county workshops or nothing. This was another turning point in my life. My passion for special needs adults had been fed since I started working in the field. But now it was not only personal, but it was becoming a passion. It was something I couldn't stop thinking about. I didn't know where this passion would lead me, but I knew I had to do something. I saw a need and started to figure out a way to create something that will fill it.

Little did I know, this was the beginning of Dreamshine.

I had a plan and it was time to act. My brother purchased a rundown campground and was working hard to renovate it. We talked and I convinced him to let me use the grounds. I did my homework and searched the Internet for places that already existed with the same programming I was envisioning. I found a website of a therapeutic program that served the special needs community, and it wasn't county owned and operated. I called the owner and explained to him what I was doing and what I wanted to do. We talked and visited. This program was the first one in Ohio to offer a choice to families with adults with special needs. I wanted to be the second one. And in our conversations, I learned that I needed to become educated about so many things: state rules and regulations, individual rights, and politics. I needed to learn how funding works and how it is set up for programs like the one I was dreaming of creating. Because these types of programs are elevated levels of adult daycare, the funding comes through Medicaid and Medicare. Up to this point, the county workshops were the only ones certified to offer services. As a result, these programs controlled the large amounts of money that came into the state. I read and read and read. I became an expert at the rules and regulations. I knew all about funding and licenses and certifications. And after a year, I became a certified and licensed agency.

Here's what I learned.

I learned that it takes building courage to get out there. It takes bravery to make decisions using the most information and the best knowledge you can. Even when you know that nothing is 100 percent guaranteed and that you may never get confirmation from anyone else, you do it anyway. I learned that I had to do that for myself in order to make my dream shine. I am proof that perseverance and passion pay off. I learned that needing and getting other people's approval is a form of fear that, like procrastination, paralyzes. In learning to navigate the system, I had at one time or another, people who helped me. But, I recognized that ultimately it all fell on my shoulders. In the end it was me who had to make the final decisions. That taught me to be brave enough. It taught me to trust my gut, work hard, and know that some people might not like my decision or what I was doing.

And that's okay.

I post quotes all the time and inspirational videos online. Some people like them. Some people don't. Someday, when I am better at speaking in front of groups, I may look back at these early videos and laugh at how terrible they are. The point is that I am not afraid to be terrible. Let me repeat that because it is very important.

I AM NOT AFRAID TO BE TERRIBLE.

My fear no longer leads me. I am led by my heart and my passion. I am led by my bigger why, which is my desire to help people. I am beyond what others think. If someone looks at what I have done and says I could have done this better or should have done it this way, I will certainly consider their opinions, learn from any constructive criticism people share with me, and perfect what I do, but I am not going to let it stop me. I refuse to let it stop me. I refuse to allow it to make me feel bad. As long as I stay true to my motivation – helping people – then I know I cannot and will not be stopped.

Getting Dreamshine up and running was one of the hardest things I've ever had to do. I made mistakes, but I learned from them. I started out knowing very little about what I needed to do, but I worked as hard as I could and learned as much as I needed to and I grew. And I will continue to grow. That's what's so great about refusing to let what others think and say stop you. Through the process of building Dreamshine, I became brave. Brave enough to make decisions that may or may not be the best. Brave enough to hold onto my intentions and stand strong while I make mistakes and decisions. This is something I had to learn to do and something I plan to continue to improve on. This is something you can learn to do, too. This is where being a solid dude starts. This is a good time for me to introduce you to Mr. Solid Dude.

Mr. Solid Dude knows that being brave and having the courage to work hard, follow through, and trust your why means being bigger than your doubts and fears. It means trusting yourself enough to overcome the odds and get to where you want to go. Mr. Solid Dude knows that you might make the wrong choice. He isn't afraid of that. He knows that he will learn from the mistakes he makes and grow into a more knowledgeable, more confident, more giving person than he was before.

That's what it means to have vision – TO HAVE A WHY. According to dictionary.com, a visionary is "a person who is given to audacious, highly speculative, or impractical ideas or schemes."[6] Basically… a dreamer. Having the dream first is important, but I would not call what I have done a scheme or an impractical idea. People who tried to stop me in the beginning were well-meaning, I'm sure, and just looking out for me. As I get further into the story behind Dreamshine, you will understand what I mean. The struggles and battles I had to choose and win were difficult and draining. If I didn't have my initial dream, I may have given up. If I didn't have the desire and passion to create something that would help so many people who have very little choices in life, I would not have become as brave and steadfast as I am today. Believe me, the journey was long and winding. That's why the word visionary just doesn't cut it. I created Mr. Solid Dude to help make my message clear. He is not a visionary. Like me, he is a visioneer.

Being a visioneer means focusing on the end result. The laser focus I learned to develop helped me through the struggles and battles with well-meaning friends who tried to talk me down and with one high-level state official who told me point-blank to quit and that what I was trying to do was impossible and that I would fail. I was threatened and told not to open Dreamshine.

Imagine working as hard as you can and learning as much as you can about something that you believed in with all of your heart and then getting close and being told to stop because you were never going to make it. Imagine how that would feel. For me, it was like crossing a mountain range. There were ups and downs, failures and successes. But, with each peak that I scaled, I became stronger and more accomplished. I knew more, felt better about where I was headed, and trusted my gut more. The small victories added up and gave me the strength to power through and cross what I like to call the sea of fear and impossibility. I saw my hard work begin to pay off. I saw how reading gave me knowledge and how important and crucial it was to apply that knowledge. I combined my character with the application of that knowledge and discovered a formula for success: Character = Knowledge x Application^2.

Solid's Theory of Wisdom

$$C = KA^2$$

key: C = Character
K = knowledge
A = Application

by Mark Minard

In other words, building a strong character that can withstand everything and anything that can and will get in the way of success means gaining the knowledge necessary and then multiplying it by application times two. That's how important application is. And that's exactly what I had to learn to do – and did – to build, hire staff, and open Dreamshine.

Welcome to Solid's Elevational Journey.

On his trip to his vision manifested, Mr. Solid Dude crosses his own seemingly insurmountable mountain range. He scales those mountains of fear and failure fueled by knowledge and double doses of application. He digs in and climbs to the top where he deals with whatever gets in his way. His vision remains laser focused as he battles storms, setbacks, and self-doubt. Mr. Solid Dude is named that because it is who he is. His character is solid and he remains fixed on reaching his goal. All of those storms, setbacks, and times of self-doubt dissolve as he reaches deep within himself. In fact, each trial he faces makes his resolve stronger and makes him braver. So strong and brave that he can cross the final hurdles of fear and impossibility to reach his goal – his vision manifested.

And that, my friends, is what a visioneer does.

In case you haven't figured it out, yet, Mr. Solid Dude is me and I can't wait to tell you the rest of how Dreamshine became a reality. Through my journey to this wonderful place for people with special needs, I have learned that being a leader means standing up for what you believe in and fighting for it. Period.

Being a leader means being a solid dude.

ON BEING INTENTIONAL

> *"It is a mistake to look too far ahead. Only one link in the chain of destiny can be handled at a time."*
> —**Winston Churchill** (1874-1965)

One of the many things I have learned in building Dreamshine is that hanging on to my comfort zone, my fears, and my circumstances will hold me back. Mr. Solid Dude agrees. He knows that at the root of his indecision is fear disguised as comfort. Mr. Solid Dude knows that in order to move ahead in life, you have to burn your security blanket. And that means being brave enough to get rid of the things that hold you back emotionally.

What's your security blanket?

In 1952, Americans met a little boy named Linus van Pelt. He was a lot smarter than most of the other kids in the Peanuts gang and was both a philosopher and theologian. Linus had to deal with an older sister, Lucy, and a younger brother, Rerun. He was Charlie Brown's best friend and is almost never seen without his blue security blanket. Charles M Schulz created Linus as a bright, well-informed, yet insecure character. Linus did not let the fact that the other kids teased him for dragging around his blanket bother him, and he was almost never seen without it. Imagine if everyone could see your emotional insecurities in the form of a blanket that you carried with you wherever you went? It would certainly make us feel less like we were the only ones with emotional baggage. The point I am trying to make here is that it is not abnormal to face self-doubts and fears. When I was about a year into creating Dreamshine, I experienced these on a whole different level of intensity. I couldn't sleep many nights because I was overwhelmed with EVERYTHING. Once I allowed myself to dwell on my thoughts, they would quickly spiral out of control. I'd become extremely anxious. The funny thing was, it was happening when things were going great, as well as when things were terrible. Any form of stress seemed to create anxiety that kept me up all night. Without the proper amount of sleep, my fears would be perpetuated and they would come back in greater force the next time I let them in. It was this continuous series of battles that led me to really think about what it means to be intentional.

And learning about myself and coming up with my own theory about it changed everything.

> *"At the root of indecision – paralyzation – is fear disguised as comfort."*

Basically, we are all under ongoing attack by the inner thoughts of our own minds. I call these thoughts attacks from the enemy. I have discovered that when my mind is idle, the attacks occur by default. The enemy will stop at nothing. He does not want you or I to succeed. By going into battle with the enemy unprepared, you will lose. And by losing, I mean you will quit or do something even worse than quitting. And the thing that's worse than quitting is being paralyzed by choice and never starting to make your elevational journey. That means not allowing yourself to take that leap. It means being so indecisive that you become stuck and immobile. Ultimately that leads to fear. Fear leads to anxiety. And soon you are dragging around a big blue security blanket and unable to move forward.

This is a great time to mention my sister, Amy Minard. Amy moved here from Portland, Oregon right around the time I was getting ready to open Dreamshine. I had already told her about the horrible workshops and lack of options for individuals with special needs. I told her everything I wanted to do and why. Amy immediately aligned herself with my vision. She had worked as a case manager for troubled teens for seven years and held a B.A. in Psychology and wanted to go all in with me. I asked her to be a partner and co-owner and she agreed to be a part of Dreamshine. Because I do not believe in coincidence, I knew that God brought us together at the perfect time.

In getting Dreamshine up and running, I have learned that making an elevational journey is a clear and intentional choice. There is no excuse for allowing the enemy to paralyze you and prevent you from succeeding at what you want to do. I am living proof that you can fight this battle and win. Creating Dreamshine is a perfect example of how to not allow fear to become so comfortable that it paralyzes. I can't imagine where all of these wonderful people would be or what they would be doing if I allowed myself to be overcome with indecision and anxiety. When I started, I wanted so much to create an environment where adults with special needs could enjoy their days and have lots of opportunities for educational and social growth. And ultimately, I did.

There was so much at stake.

But getting there was like walking down a long and winding road. After Amy and I got our initial certification to operate Dreamshine as a day habilitation agency, we worked toward and became certified to provide transportation. This way we get to pick up individuals who participate in our program at their homes each morning in our large passenger vehicles and then bring them back home at the end of the day. We were ready to roll. We sent out brochures and did all we could to get people to recognize that we were a viable alternative to county placement. That's when I was threatened and warned by people in high places not to open. They wanted to shut me down before I even got started.

Finally, I found out about a 23-year-old man with special needs who had been attending the county workshops and was miserable. His mother had visited the facility and witnessed firsthand just how much of nothing he was doing all day. She heard about Dreamshine and wanted her son to attend. At that time, we were officially certified, set up, and ready. This young man would have been our very first participant. But when the mother talked to the county about switching programs, they would not allow it.

Thank goodness I had done my homework. I had proof that individuals with special needs were allowed by law to attend any program they chose as long as the program was certified. Kind of like health insurance. As long as your health care provider is covered, the insurance will pay for your visits. When I found out this young man, who was so unhappy at the county workshop and was not being allowed to come to our innovative and educational program, I went right to the top. I met and argued with county and state officials and brought copies of the rules. I read them out loud. I proved that I knew what I was talking about. They knew they were wrong and they also knew that if they did not allow this young man's family to choose a better placement for him, they could be reported and investigated by the state. I stood up and they backed down. The next day, this young man – and our first participant – enrolled at Dreamshine. This was 2007. And by the end of the summer, we had seven more individuals enroll.

The issues that got in the way of our first enrollee plagued others that followed. It seemed to never end. Families from other counties began hearing about our program and wanted to send their adult children to Dreamshine, too. We stood strong when funding was withheld. We kept our heads up when dealing with fabricated audits and fake citations. We never gave up. What I did was the opposite. I dug deeper into the rules and became an advocate for the people who belonged at Dreamshine. We were literally put through hell.

What I went through while trying to get Dreamshine up and running was above-average stress, but it made me realize that giving up was never an option. The passion of my WHY – or the reason why I was pressing on - kept me going. I attended countless meetings with state officials and eventually the state rules governing programming for adults with special needs was rewritten and changed. The policy changes that were made benefitted all individuals with special needs. And I am proud to say that other programs began sprouting up.

Finally these families had a choice.

Aside from county issues, we were up to eight young adults with special needs and still sharing space at my brother's campground. Don't' get me wrong. We loved it there. Amy and I are and always will be grateful for the amazing opportunity my brother and sister-in-law gave us by allowing us to start Dreamshine at their beautiful campground. But, my office was in my brother's storage shed and when he catered a wedding or weekend event at the main building, we had to move everything from our program out of the room and then back in time for Monday morning. As a result, we started looking for a place with the same open-air feeling where we could relocate. We wanted to find an outdoorsy, campground environment that was as far from institutional-looking as we could get. Eventually we found a log home, and with the help of my parents, we bought the property and now call this home.

Flash forward eight years later, and here we are.

Creating and running Dreamshine has been challenging, and I fight my emotional insecurities every day, but it is worth everything to me. It taught me how to deal with the inner thoughts that tell me to give up. The difference between the way I was before Dreamshine and the way I am now is that now I no longer dwell on those thoughts. They still pop up, but I have figured out how to work around them. Even now, as I write this book I am haunted. Even before I started this very page, a voice inside my mind told me that I can't do this. It shouted that no one would ever want to read my story. It sneered that I am wasting my time. But like I said before – and this is the game-changer – I have learned not to dwell and obsess on them. Where I used to have a conversation with these thoughts and allow them to convince me that they were true, I now say, "No more!" But before I share my trade secrets, let's go back to Linus and his blanket for a few more minutes.

> *"It doesn't matter if you are an entrepreneur, a mom, dad, parent, teacher, or assistant, serve your clients and fellow workers. Keep growing and doing your best. Your life will change along the way..."*

Linus had brains, wit and insight, but the first thing we saw was a big blue blanket. Like the equivalent of wearing your heart on your sleeve, that blanket was a visual reminder that Linus was insecure.

So what color is your blanket?

Like I said, we all have fears or anxieties or thoughts that can interfere with our success. Knowing that we all feel afraid, apprehensive, or unsure sometimes is a bit of a comfort. The important thing about this is that we don't let it strangle us. A security blanket that everyone

can see sends a message. It's kind of like saying every thought that comes
into your head out loud.

"I can't do this."

"No one will ever want to read this book."

"I should just give up."

"Who am I to think I can do this better than someone else?"

Like Linus' blanket, saying our thoughts out loud is a way for people
to see that we are not completely sure that we are going to accomplish
the thing we are setting out to do. There's something about entrusting
a person who does not believe in himself with a task that requires
confidence and motivation. Susan Baroncini-Moe writes for Lifehack.
com. She has been writing for the website, which provides information
and tips on a range of topics including business, life, relationships and
money, since January 2009. In her article, "Change the Way You See
Fear and Change Your Life," Baroncini-Moe says that once we get
comfortable, we stay that way for as long as we can. It's how we are
programmed. But in order to move ahead in life, we must fight those
feelings and the way we have become programmed. In fact, according
to the article, "fear is the number one reason why people stay in their
comfort zones."[7] For Linus, his blanket is his comfort zone. He can form
it into any shape he wants. For example, in various comic strips, Linus'
blanket became a scarf, a quilt for Lucy's doll's bed, a parachute, sports
coats for both he and Snoopy, a bullfighter's cape, a whip, a slingshot,
and second base, to name a few. He functions well with his blanket,
and does not function at all without it. But beginning in April of 1983,
Linus learns how to survive without his beloved security blanket. And
once cured, he begins to share his success story and how he did it with
anyone who would listen.[8]

I am a lot like Linus. Even though I never carried around a big blue
blanket, I had my own version of a security blanket. It was fear and
anxiety. I knew I needed to learn to deal with my thoughts and feelings,

but never really knew what to do. It wasn't until I began working for a cause, a belief, a passion, that I recognized that I could function just fine – and even exceed my own expectations – without that security blanket of fear holding me down. I learned how get rid of my blanket. I no longer have the conversation I used to have with these thoughts. I no longer allow the enemy to convince me that what I am thinking is true. As a result, I no longer allow myself to be controlled and paralyzed by my fears and anxieties and indecisiveness. And here's how I do it in two steps:

Step ONE: Awareness The first thing I do is recognize when the enemy is attacking. I already know what it feels like. I am idle and suddenly my mind is a whirling tornado of chaos and my thoughts are spinning out of control. One thought seems to fuel the next. If I allow them to continue, soon I have a wildfire. But like me, you can learn how to recognize an oncoming invasion.

Thoughts that prevent you from doing what you need and want to do usually end up focusing you on the worst possible scenarios. Your fears are driving the way your mind sees your outcomes. For example, if in the middle of all of the hard things that were happening while creating Dreamshine I allowed my negative thoughts to play out - and don't get me wrong, sometimes they did – I would have been telling myself at 2 a.m. that this was a crazy idea and it is not realistic to continue pursuing it. The fears that kept me up at night would have eventually changed the way I envisioned Dreamshine.

Alan Alda is an American actor most known for his role as Hawkeye Pierce in the television series M*A*S*H*. He says, "You have to leave the city of your comfort and go into the wilderness of your intuition. What you'll discover will be wonderful. What you'll discover is yourself."[9] I find this to be true because once I began fighting the enemy, I learned more about who I am and what I am capable of accomplishing. This leads to the second step.

Step TWO: Counteraction   When I am overcome by the enemy, I counteract these thoughts with the TRUTH. For me, the truth is what God has told me. I focus on God's words by either thinking about them or yelling them out loud. Please note that this is not something I recommend unless you are alone. (You don't want to look completely crazy.) My life now is so busy and I thank God every day for all he has given me, both good and bad. And when the bad hits, like my obsessive thoughts and fears, I go to him for guidance.

In 2 Timothy 1:7, it says, "For the Spirit God gave us does not make us timid, But gives us power, love and self-discipline." Isn't this great? What God is saying here is so plain and simple to me. God is telling me to stand up and fight for the strengths he has given me. He is telling me to control my thoughts and know that I can fight the enemy. I repeat this Bible scripture over and over until I can feel the power of the words building inside of me. It is then that I realize that I must choose to believe this truth. It is then that I know that everything else is a lie. My fears are lies. My anxieties are lies. That voice in my head that is telling me to quit is a lie. God's words here are like a sword of truth that I can use to strike the enemy down. By declaring the verse from 2 Timothy, either out loud or in my mind, I counterattack the enemy and knock him flat on his back. God gives us many, many verses like this one that gives good advice about not living in fear and the power we have in him. (All you have to do is use an online Bible search program to find them.) But the bottom line is that God does not want us to be afraid. He made us fearless and gives us the power to defeat the enemy.

Mr. Solid Dude has his own way of dealing with his security blanket, too. He says to burn it. Get rid of it. Solid knows that fear can be disguised as comfort and when things get too comfortable, it's hard to change. Sometimes the best thing to do is something drastic.

Burn your security blanket.

Courage comes from kicking down the walls of comfort that are built up by fear. This is important to remember. Having the courage to stand up to your fears and anxieties and negative thoughts is an intentional act. Everything I do and say and think must be intentional. In order for me to achieve my goals and continue my dream at Dreamshine I must be intentional. And before I can teach you how to be intentional, it is vital to understand what that means.

"Courage is manifested by kicking down the walls of comfort built by fear."

According to Merriam Webster's online dictionary and thesaurus, the word intentional means "done by intention or design, with an aim or purpose." Its synonyms include words like deliberate, purposeful, conscious, and intended.[10] These are all things that require thought and mindfulness. Being intentional means not only fighting the battle on the inside, but doing things on the outside that help pull you along, as well.

Rick Warren is an expert on living a life with purpose. And doing things in an intentional way is living a life purposefully. In fact in 2002, Rick Warren wrote a book entitled, *The Purpose Driven Life.* The book is meant to be read over the course of 40 days. Each chapter focuses on one thing that will transform your life. Unlike a self-help book, Warren's devotional makes you think about and start with God. In fact, Warren states in his opening chapter that "one reason most books don't transform us is that we are so eager to read the next chapter, we don't pause and take the time to seriously consider what we have just read. We rush to the next truth without reflecting on what we have learned."[11] So he recommends reading one chapter per day, interacting with and annotating the book as you read, and reacting to what is said. Warren believes that everything starts with God. One of the hundreds of scripture verses quoted in the book is from Romans 12:2. It says, "…let God transform you into a new person by changing the way you think. Then you will learn to know God's will for you, which is good and pleasing and perfect." (NLT) Warren believes that life is a gift, that it is a test, and that it is our temporary assignment. Rick Warren and his wife, Kay, co-founded the Saddleback megachurches in California. At the tenth anniversary of its publication, *The Purpose Driven Life* has sold more than 32 million copies around the world in 50 different languages. The reason I bring it up is because living in an intentional way means living with purpose of thought. And that means living the way God wants us to live: fearlessly fighting the enemy and working to help others. And that is what I am going to help you learn to do. I am proof that living in an intentional way works. If I hadn't intentionally fought the enemy on a daily basis and allowed my fear to overtake my thoughts and my life, you would not be reading this book today.

My sister, Amy, and I had a powerful partnership and fought in the trenches together from 2007 to 2014. We may have disagreed at times, but we always agreed on the same overall mission, core values, and principles of Dreamshine. We both have Christ as our foundation and have great respect for each other. Through the mistakes and times when we lost our tempers with each other, that respect carried us through. It takes a lot of work and intentional communication to make such an awesome team. We learned from our mistakes and made sure to have the courageous conversations in order to help each other grow.

Dreamshine always came first.

As of October 2014, Amy followed her heart and began a new adventure in Ethiopia. She had already adopted two children from there and continued to feel a calling and pulling at her gut to go to Ethiopia to work with orphans and individuals with special needs. After months of soul-searching, Amy made the decision to leave Dreamshine. Even though she was happy with everything she was doing at Dreamshine and her life in Ohio, she could not deny the pulling at her gut that would not go away. I remember the day she came into my office, in tears, and announced that she was moving to Ethiopia to work as a volunteer administrator at the Grace Center. When we were kids, my sister talked about wanting to help children in Africa. I knew it was only a matter of time when she would make that happen. Plus, I would never stand in the way of what God was calling her to do. This was her new WHY and she had to go.

This is a great way to show you how your WHY and vision and dreams can change, grow, and develop over time. In Ecclesiastes 3:1, the Bible says "To every thing there is a season, and a time to every purpose under heaven." It was time. My sister's new season was upon her. She was courageously embarking on a whole new and unknown adventure that was out of her comfort zone. She said yes to Jesus and joined Him as He called her. (For information about Amy's ministry, please go to http://minardsatgracecenter.weebly.com).

Before Amy left, we made a plan where I would take over full ownership of Dreamshine. She has been gone for about 10 months. As I write this book, I can say that it has been a hard adjustment all around – for Amy and the rest of us here. But, Amy is following what God's plan is for her life and as a result, so much good is being done.

Not too long ago, Amy emailed me to tell me about a baby who was brought to her. The baby was not breathing and everyone was screaming and crying. Amy grabbed the baby and immediately began CPR. She had never done CPR on a live child before. But she did not hesitate and as a result, the baby began to breathe and cry. My sister saved that baby's life. I love my sister and am sad that she is not at Dreamshine, but I have the utmost respect for her on every level.

I thank God every day for his grace. He brought Amy and I together to create Dreamshine. He called her to ministry in Ethiopia and left me here to become the leader I am today.

God is my WHY. I thank you for buying my book and reading it. I hope it helps you. You are my WHY. And I want to do all I can to help you learn to live an intentional life.

But before we get to that, you have to get to your WHY first.

WHY WE NEED A WHY

"Change your mindset and your circumstances will follow."
—Mark Minard

E arlier in the book I said that it takes building a type of courage and bravery to put yourself and your stuff out there. It takes courage to make decisions with the best knowledge you have knowing that in the end nothing is 100 percent guaranteed. You need to be brave to live with the fact the no one is going to confirm everything for you. And it takes guts to learn that lesson and do that for yourself.

Being intentional and being willing are two huge words I associate with my success and the success of Dreamshine. Learning to apply being intentional and willing can mean the difference between success and failure in your life.

"Reach up in the sky and pull your dream down.
Then you will find where vision is found!"
—Mr. Solid Dude

Solid's message about knowing the course you want to take is tied closely to what I call my WHY.

In my illustration below, you see Solid. He is climbing a ladder to reach his dream. Once he gets to the top of the ladder and his dream is realized, Solid can come back down to the ground and formulate his vision. Solid believes that he must first envision and grasp a dream before he can create his vision to move forward. And like my dream to create a caring and supportive environment for adults with special needs where there wasn't one before, Solid believes that anything is possible.

Study that illustration carefully because you are going to draw your own illustration now. Think about why you are reading this book. You obviously are interested in learning how to be better, accomplish a dream, become a serving leader, or just figure out what it is you want to do in life. Use the template below and instead of Solid, draw yourself. Think about what your dream is. And where the word dream is in my illustration, replace it with exactly what it is you want to do or become. Then draw yourself again on the ground. Like Solid, you believe that anything is possible. Like Solid, you will have a vision to accompany your dream. If you have already taken steps toward creating your vision, make notes on your illustration. Mark it up. Make it yours. This is something that I am asking you to do because it is the first step in making intentional choices to abandon and walk away from the voices in your head that are telling you that are not good enough.

Not smart enough.

Not ready enough.

Go ahead. Put yourself into the illustration. Ponder. Think. Dream. It's good for you. And where there is a big box at the end of the vision, go ahead and write down exactly where you want to go or do or be or create.

What Solid is trying to get you to understand is that you have to be willing to focus on what you want and take one intentional step at a time to get there. Intentional living is mostly about fighting the battle with the enemy. Sometimes it seems like the series of battles are becoming one big war, but don't give up. Once you win that war, you will never be the same again.

Ever.

My dream for creating Dreamshine became my WHY. I saw the alternative for families and believed in my heart that there had to be a better way for these wonderfully-made adults to spend their days. I was haunted by the images in my brain of the institutionalized drudgery and nonexistent interaction. I was moved in my heart to do something. Even if it meant hours and hours and hours of sleepless nights. Even if it meant endless meetings and hearings and disappointments. I never lost sight of my dream. And I never lost sight of my vision. And that vision was to "ensure the highest quality of independence, personal growth, and social interaction for individuals with special needs." I was determined to provide a safe and caring environment where participants can have fun while exploring new interests and activities on campus and out in the community.

I've done that. And I attribute much of how I got there to my belief and faith in God, my intentional living, and three more things:

1. I read books of wisdom written by leaders.
2. I listen to strong leaders speak.
3. I surround myself with like-minded people.

I know I told you how reading changed my life. Well, it is still changing my life. I am busy, but I know how important it is to read what others have written on topics that can help me continue to grow and succeed. One book that has meant a lot to me is entitled, *Outwitting the Devil.* It was written in 1938 by Napoleon Hill (1883-1970), who was one of the first authors to write successfully about how to achieve personal success. Hill's list of books is long and notable. In *Outwitting the Devil,* Hill writes, "Fear is the tool of a man-made devil. Self-confident faith in one's self is both the man-made weapon which defeats this devil and the man-made tool which builds a triumphant life. And it is more than that. It is a link to the irresistible forces of the universe which stand behind a man who does not believe in failure and defeat as being anything but temporary experiences."[12] Hill nails it. Not only does he talk about how fear and other self-harming thoughts, like procrastination and anger, prevent us from achieving our dreams, but he also outlines how we can win against those thoughts that I call the enemy.

I highly recommend that you read this book.

I also listen to Joel Osteen preach. Osteen is an American preacher, author and senior pastor of Lakewood Church in Houston, Texas. Lakewood is currently the largest Protestant Church in America and Osteen's televised sermons are viewed by more than seven million people each week. His first book, *Your Best Life Now,* was written in 2004, and he has since gone on to write more. In fact, five of his books have been included on the *New York Times* bestseller list. Osteen's books are self-help in nature and deal with topics that range from living a fulfilled life to achieving your goals to getting unstuck when you can't seem to move forward. Osteen's sermons are filled with passion and everyday examples of how to live the way God wants us to. Find him on the Internet and listen.

The third way I fight the enemy is by connecting with a handful of like-minded people who I pull closely into what I call my mastermind group. This group is made up of about five people who range in age and areas of success, such as marriage, faith, children, finances, and so on. They also are people who are doing the same type of things that I am doing. My mastermind group encourages me and I encourage them. We help hold each other accountable and speak wisdom to each other. Our main purpose is to help each other grow. That's because we all speak the truth, even if it hurts to say or hear it. I know that in order to elevate growth in any area of my own life, I need these like-minded people to help me stay on track.

I know it is important to know God. And they do, too. I know it is vital to equip myself with a "sword" so that no matter what, I can fight back and overcome the enemy.

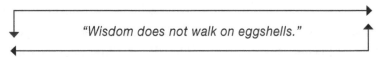

"Wisdom does not walk on eggshells."

This group helps me do that. I suggest you start pulling together a group like this. It can be made up of your spouse, a mentor, and like-minded friends. But, it has to be people who will work in unity and help you gain the power to find success. The beauty of mentoring is hard to explain. But when others are willing to help you and you are willing to help them back, intentional living becomes a natural consequence.

Take a moment and write down the names of a few people who you might talk to about your dream and who you might consider asking if he or she is interested in forming a mastermind group.

_____

_____

_____

The three things I outlined above – reading wise authors, listening to strong leaders, and working with like-minded people – are three of the ways that I use to keep me going strong. Another way is to focus on my WHY. Even now, things are sometimes hard. When that happens, I take out a piece of paper and begin writing what would happen if I were to quit now.

Think about a time when things were difficult or really challenging. Think about how hard it was or is. Make a list of who would be affected if you quit, gave up, and walked away. Think about all of the ways people would be affected, not just the financial implications of quitting. Think about the emotional implications, too. Think about every single way your decision to quit what you believe in would affect everyone involved. Then write that list here:

1. _____
2. _____
3. _____
4. _____
5. _____

Now let it go for. While it is beneficial to look at what might happen if you give up, the important and real takeaway of this very brief exercise is that you don't want it to happen. You don't really want to give. You don't want to negatively affect the lives of your employees, friends, family, and clients. And most of all, you cannot afford to negatively affect your own life in this way. To analyze what would happen if you quit would mean investing time and energy into the "what if." And this takes time away from the here and now. Even a few minutes of allowing yourself to think about quitting is a few minutes too many. We all have obstacles that we have to overcome. It is a part of growing and learning. It is a part of life.

Because it's been a part of my life, too, I can share with you how I keep going. In fact, instead of rehashing the challenges and negative experiences that brought me to the point of even considering giving it all up, our time in this book together is better spent thinking about the WHY and the HOW of moving forward.

I hope you agree.

OVERCOMING

"What if? And I said, 'It won't.'"
—Mark Minard

There's an old saying that tells us that when the going gets tough, the tough get going. I have my own take on this. I believe that we have to be willing to take a chance or a risk, and that's what the definition of tough is. In order to move Dreamshine out of my head and into the world where it would help so many people, I had to be willing to put it all out there. I had to be willing to put myself way out there. Despite the challenges and the struggles, I am still out there. Dreamshine is still proudly serving people with special needs. As I said before, when the thought of throwing in the towel crosses my mind, I pause and think about what if.

What if I quit.

What if I just walk away and allow the hard stuff to swallow me whole and paralyze me.

What if I lost sight of my WHY and turned my back on my dream.

I am here to say that we all have moments like this. We all have fears and obstacles to overcome. Life is hard, but I have learned that quitting is not an option. Not for me. Not for you. So how do I get past these times when things look bleak and dark? Let me tell you about something that happened to me recently.

I have been posting inspirational quotes and pictures online for a while and keeping track of the interest in them. One day someone contacted me about what I was posting. He thought the quotes I was sharing were creative and inspirational. He wanted to help and we worked for a few months on this amazing project. We were excited about getting started and began announcing it publicly. A landing page was created for it and it was generating a lot of interest. One week before the launch of our first webinar/podcast, I received an email informing me that it was no longer a go. No explanation. I was canceled before we even got off the ground. And because they chose not to announce it publicly, I had to let the people who had been signing up for the webinar know that my plans had fallen through. I had to apologize for something that was not my decision. In my world, when I am in a situation where something falls through, or cannot happen, I take responsibility for it. I believe I am accountable to the people who are affected by what happened. The decision that was made to cancel the webinar and how it was communicated to me went against everything I taught and shared about character and leadership. I would have offered a series of solutions and then publicly made an apology. That would have been followed up with a plan of action of how I would offer another show and when. This time, however, it was out of my control.

But guess what? Once I got through the disappointment and being upset about the cancelation, things changed. I can't honestly say here that

I didn't fall into a few moments where I took on the victim's mindset. Because I did. After all, I did have a valid reason and every right to feel upset. But I also had the right to take control of my own reaction. I am always in control of me.

I am ALWAYS in control of ME.

So I decided to keep DOING. At the time, I did not know the how, but I still had my WHY. It was my WHY that propelled me further. It kept me going. And then, three months later, I teamed up with Dayne Gingrich, a former athlete. We began talking and decided to create and co-host a series of leadership podcasts offering real life wisdom about overcoming adversity and helping whomever listens to achieve success on every level of life. We were thinking about sharing our own personal and true stories of hitting rock bottom in life, sports, work, marriage, and family. And on December 11, 2014, we launched our podcast series, "Elevating Beyond with Mark and Dayne." In two months, our podcasts have been downloaded more than 20,000 times. In just six months, our podcast has been downloaded more than 100,000 times. We have had some incredible guests on the show so far, with many more to come. It is free on iTunes and can also be found at www.hipcast.com.

Writing this book and co-hosting our podcast series has been huge for me. In fact, it has helped me realize how everything in my life - Dreamshine, this book, the podcasts – are connected to three words that make up one huge phrase: God is orchestrating. Coming to this realization was big for me. It has become one of the tools I rely on when obstacles present themselves in my life.

GOD IS THE GREAT ORCHESTRATOR

"But Jesus looked at them and said, "With man this is impossible, but with God all things are possible."
—Matthew 19:26 (ESV)

now know that God is orchestrating my life and my vision. And knowing this has changed everything about the way I look at what I do. I realize that what I do is not an obligation. I did not create Dreamshine because I felt obligated to provide services for adults with special needs. I am not the husband and father I am out of obligation. I am not writing or recording podcasts because I feel required to do them. Because I know that God is arranging, coordinating, managing, composing, and symphonizing everything in my life, I do everything in my life out of honor and duty. Because of knowing that God is orchestrating my life, I know that I have been called to do the things I do. This feeling of being called is the underlying foundation of my WHY.

We all have reasons why we do the things we do. We could choose to dwell on the negative aspect of every challenge we face, or we can choose to use it. In the case of the person who at the last minute canceled my webinars, I was initially dwelling on how I felt, but that changed after I separated the person who made the decision from their behavior. Once I did that, I was able to forgive, give it to God, and then move forward.

Negative people are like garbage trucks filled with trash. They need to find a place to dump their garbage. When you happen to be that place, it is important to make sure the trash stays on their truck. It is up to you to see to it that they take their garbage with them when they leave. In other words, I may have felt very disappointed and wronged after being told that the webinar was not going to happen, but once I made the decision to get over it and move on, the garbage went back on the truck when the truck drove away.

Forgiveness is a wonderful thing.

I need to forgive others because every day, God forgives me. And forgiving other people is not only about the other person, but it is about me and my own spiritual growth. I'm not making this up, Read the Bible and you will see that in Colossians 3:13, it says, "Bear with each other and forgive one another if any of you has a grievance against someone. Forgive as the Lord forgave you." And in Luke 6:37, Jesus says, "Do not judge, and you will not be judged. Do not condemn, and you will not be condemned. Forgive, and you will be forgiven." But the interesting thing about that verse in Luke is that Jesus goes on to say, "Give, and it will be given to you. A good measure, pressed down, shaken together and running over, will be poured into your lap. For with the measure you use, it will be measured to you."

In other words, forgive because you will need to be forgiven someday. Forgive because God has already forgiven you. Cool, right?

I went through one of the darkest times of my life about six years ago. Everything in my life was in trouble: My marriage, my family, my business, my life. It was a time when I came to a place where I realized I did not have the power to fix everything. In fact, I was at a point where I could fix nothing that was going wrong in my life. One afternoon, after an excruciatingly difficult time, I got down on my knees on the floor. It was January in Ohio at about 4 p.m. It was getting dark. It was cold and the skies were gray. I got down on the floor and looked up. With tears streaming down my face, one by one I handed everything to God: My life. My kids. My marriage. My business. All of it. I had come to the place where I had recognized that I no longer had control.

No control at all.

I prayed to God and knew that only he could take my life, my marriage, my kids, and my business and be in control of it all. With faith and trust, and having no idea what the outcome would be, I gave everything to God. That first step on the floor in a small apartment in January changed my life. I figured out that there was no better place for everything that was going on with me than in the hands of God. And so as I gave each of the things that mattered in my life to him, I began to feel a powerful wave of peace come over me. I had admitted to God that I couldn't do any of things in my life without him. I gave it all up and trusted that he would help me.

That's what faith and trust means.

Since that afternoon, things have not been perfect, but I walk every day knowing that God is in control, not me. I have since been baptized and as a family, we continue to walk toward God. There really is no other option. So when I say that I let that negative experience of having someone cancel my webinar at the last minute go, now you understand how I can do that. God really is the great orchestrator.

Not too long after that experience, I went on to co-host an awesome podcast series with Dayne. And the whole experience taught me that life is all about choosing to respond or not respond to people or circumstances that are negative and out of your control. It is about making an intentional choice to let the negativity wash over you and past you. It's making sure that garbage truck takes its trash when it leaves. It's about perspective and Solid has a lot to say about that.

SPAM

"It's easy to get negative because you get beat down. You go through a few disappointments and it's easy to stay in that negative frame of mind. Choosing to be positive and having a grateful attitude is a whole cliché, but your attitude is going to determine how you're going to live your life."
—**Joel Osteen**

Spam is defined in the Urban Dictionary like this:
spam spam spam spam spam spam spam spam spam spam spam spam spam spam spam spam spam spam spam spam spam spam spam spam spam spam spam spam spam spam spam spam spam spam spam spam spam spam spam spam spam spam spam spam spam spam spam spam spam spam spam spam spam spam spam spam spam spam spam spam spam spam spam spam spam spam spam spam spam spam spam spam

spam spam spam spam spam spam spam spam spam spam spam spam
spam spam spam spam spam spam spam spam spam spam spam spam
spam spam spam spam spam spam spam spam spam spam spam spam
spam spam spam spam spam spam

"This is what span is. Would be better without it."[13]

According to a survey of 1,055 adults conducted by "The Online Privacy Blog," the average adult gets about 105 unwanted emails every day. This is spam. And according to this blog, there are five ways to avoid getting spam emails. Here are three of them:

1. You can create a "fake" email address that you use to sign up for online accounts. By not using your real, or primary email address, you avoid having to deal with spam.
2. You can filter it. This means you set up filters through your settings menu in your email account which puts certain emails into different inboxes. For example, if you create a filter and a "Spam" folder that automatically deletes unwanted emails, you do not have to deal with them. Ever.
3. You can unsubscribe to the spam emails. This is tedious work, but tends to be the easiest way to cut down on spam emails. In fact, more than half of the adults who participated in the survey said that this was their preferred way to deal with spam.[14]

Like this definition of spam, negative people, as a group, are generally repetitious, always the same, and unwanted. Like spam, they clog up your inbox, usually are not beneficial, and almost always take some kind of effort to either ignore or get rid of. If you do not remove spam from your email account, it would just keep piling up. Solid calls this negative information overload spam, too. Only he knows that if you don't file it away and get it out of sight, it can affect the way you live your life.

In my illustration below, we meet a new character. His name is Mr. Negative Face. Mr. Negative Face spends his life putting others down. As you can see, his thoughts are negative, his words are negative, and even the expression on his face is negative. He is not happy and he doesn't want people around him to be happy, either. Mr. Negative Face is not worth spending a lot of time on because if you look carefully at the illustration, Solid has already filed his negativity away in what he calls his "Cerebral Spam Folder for Negative People." He is smiling because he has figured out a way to not allow Mr. Negative Face and his spam to infiltrate his thoughts.

This is what we all have to learn to do in order to achieve the success we seek in our lives. Solid chooses to file it away where it can be automatically deleted. As you can see, the closer Mr. Negative Face's words get to Solid, the smaller and more insignificant they get. By not allowing negative thoughts and words to control or get in the way with his success, Solid has created a life where he can concentrate on getting what he needs done. As we saw in an earlier illustration, Solid has learned to change his mindset so that his circumstances will follow.

I want to help you get rid of the spam that is clogging up your life. We have already talked about overcoming fear and anxieties. We talked about the importance of practicing awareness and counteraction. This is the perfect time to tell you about how to "keep doing."

Leslie Calvin "Les" Brown is an author, motivational speaker and politician. He served as a member of the Ohio House of Representatives from 1977 to 1983 and most recently teaches people how to achieve success in their lives as they follow their dreams. His catch phrase is "It's possible," but he also said, "You don't have to be great to get started, but you have to get started to be great." This is so true. And for me, getting Dreamshine started had to happen before it could be great. God knows at the beginning of the process I was far from great. But I never gave up. I worked hard and studied long hours and showed up. I knew what my dream was and got there by sheer determination and with a lot of God's help. It's the same story with the quotes I started tweeting and posting online. It's the same story with the podcast I co-host. I may not start out being all the good, but as I said before, I am not afraid of being terrible.

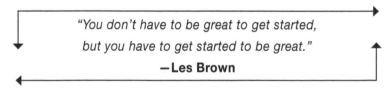

"You don't have to be great to get started,
but you have to get started to be great."
—**Les Brown**

One very specific thing I have learned to do is keep DOING. And that means exactly what it sounds like it means.

For example, a year ago I decided that I wanted to write a book. I am an extremely busy person. Between my business and my family I could have easy said that I would not be able to write this book. The conditions around creating something that I dreamed would help others were far from perfect.

But I kept DOING.

I started posting quotes on Twitter. They focused on leadership and the contents of what I would put into a book.

This book.

At the time, all I knew was that I had a book inside me that I knew would help many people live their dreams as I have. I felt passionate about getting my ideas and tools into the hands of as many people as I could.

So I kept DOING.

At around that same time, I began drawing sketches. The more I wrote, the more clearer things became to me. Mr. Solid Dude was manifested. I had no idea where the sketches would go, but I kept DOING.

Throughout this entire process I experienced fear and self-doubt. I've had setbacks and I've had to put many hours and an incredible amount of work into this book. It has taken time and lots of energy. I even had one friend share his concerns about me writing this book. His intentions were good because he knew how overwhelmed I was with Dreamshine and our new baby. But he still expressed his what ifs.

"You've never written a book. What if it fails?"

"What if you don't have enough time to finish?"

But I kept DOING.

My response to his concerns was easy. I told him that while everything he said was justified and made sense on some logical level, I had a desire and a bigger picture in mind. I told him that writing this book was placed on my heart and the decision I made to see it through was final. My bigger picture was to lead and speak and change lives. And this desire was to do it at a much higher magnitude than even I had imagined. I knew this was bigger than me. God is the author and creator of my vision. I know that if I had selfishly created it on my own, I would be as concerned as my friend was.

And so…I kept DOING.

START DOING

> *"The best two-step business plan ever:*
> *Stop planning and start doing."*
> **—Mark Minard**

Two valuable tools that have gotten me through almost every negative and adverse situation are: 1. to keep DOING and; 2. count on the fact that God is orchestrating my life. These may sound like simple directions, but as you just finished reading, it took a lot of work and struggles for me to get here. Before you can use these tools in your own journey, you have to get started DOING with what you HAVE.

As I began to tweet and post more and more inspirational quotes and pictures about leadership, I began to pay close attention to how many people were viewing them. I studied which quotes got more attention or reactions. I analyzed which drawings people liked better. I became obsessed with generating more and more material. I was coming up with quotes in my head while I showered in the morning, jogged, drove to work, and ate my lunch. All day and night I was thinking on a whole deeper level. I knew writing this book would be time-consuming, but in the process I also learned that it took believing in myself and the daily act of fighting the fear and self-doubt that can and will, at times, get in your way.

But at some point, the planning has to stop and the DOING has to start. So now it's your turn. Take a few minutes and close your eyes. Think about all the planning and obsessing that is probably going on in your head as you work your way toward where you want to be in life. Picture yourself working toward that goal. What are some of your immediate hurdles?

_____

_____

_____

Now think about what you've read so far and choose two points that resonate and have encouraged or inspired you. How are you going to put what you've read so far into action?

_____

_____

_____

And finally…where do you see yourself in five years?

_____

_____

_____

Great job. Because now it's time to start DOING.

PERSPECTIVE

"The greatest part about realizing you are the problem is discovering you are also the solution."
—**Mark Minard**

Mr. Mediocracy Face is his own worst enemy. He is scattered and incompetent. He is just average and not influential in thought, at all. In fact, his thoughts go around and around and around. Mr. Mediocracy Face is not a solid dude and more often than not, he will end up leading you nowhere. As you can see by the expression on his face, this character is clueless. He has no idea how messed up his situation is. There is no sense of urgency or order. He may or may not be happy with his life or the way things are, but he will continue to live in the middle of the road because that's what he knows.

He may or may not be negative, but he is most definitely paralyzed in the land of mediocrity. In fact, he probably doesn't even know it.

Enter a little perspective.

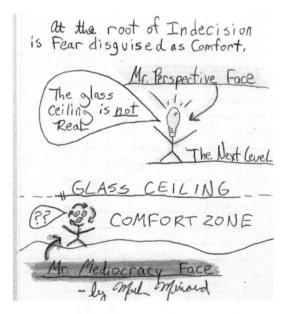

The Merriam-Webster dictionary defines the glass ceiling as an intangible barrier or an unfair system which prevents some people from getting the most powerful jobs or upper-level positions. Bottom line: The glass ceiling is a visual reminder that even though you can see through it to the next level, you cannot reach that level yourself. For Mr. Mediocracy Face, that's perfectly fine. Remember…he is happy living a life of non-meaning. It's like how Mr. Negative Face only focuses on the negative. All he sees are the problems and the obstacles that are in the way. More often than not, Mr. Negative Face acts like a victim to his circumstances and is always saying only if.

"Only if this would happen."

"Only if this would change."

With Mr. Negative Face, there is no personal accountability. But it's that way for Mr. Mediocracy Face, too. You see, he tends to fall victim to every circumstance and also does not respect accountability. However, there is hope. Mr. Perspective Face is the light bulb in this room.

I have learned that perspective is everything. In the above illustration, the glass ceiling divides two worlds. There is comfort in Mr. Mediocracy Face's world. But we learned earlier in this book that sometimes we have to be uncomfortable to grow.

"At the root of indecision is fear disguised as comfort."

Notice how the glass ceiling divides the worlds between comfort and the next level. In order to take your dreams to the next level, you have to be like Mr. Perspective Face and realize that the glass ceiling is not real. It is merely an invisible dividing line that separates those who are serious about achieving their goals and those who are happy right where they are.

Or think they are.

THE REAL WORLD

"This is the true story...of seven strangers...picked to live in a house...work together and have their lives taped...to find out what happens...when people stop being polite...and start getting real..."
—The Real World

I n 1992, MTV launched America's first reality TV series. It was a fairly new genre for Americans and ended up being the longest-running program in the history of MTV. In fact, the show started its 30th season at the end of 2014. The series throws together a diverse group of twenty-somethings and in between the drunkenness and obnoxious behavior, there's lots of discussions and disagreements about sex and sexuality, illness and death, politics, religion and substance abuse. You name it, one of the show's guests have struggled with it.

And talked about it.

They laugh. They cry. They fight. They make up.

The Real World has been called the pioneer of reality television. And in an article in *The Daily News,* fans of the show worship it. And those who aren't fans, leave the room.[15] I know the title of the show implies that it's about living in the real world, but as far as I'm concerned, no one in my real world acts like that.

Let's imagine our own reality show.

(Mr. Solid Dude and Mr. Perspective Face are sitting at the kitchen table drinking coffee and reading. Solid is planning to leave for work in 10 minutes. In walks Mr. Negative Face.)

"Is that what you plan to wear today? I thought you had a big presentation at work?" chides Mr. Negative Face.

(Solid looks up from his newspaper and nods.) "I do," he says. "Thanks for remembering."

(Mr. Negative Face seems confused.) "Ummm. Yeah. Right," he stammers. "Are you sure you're ready? What if you can't answer their questions?"

"I'm good," Solid says. *(still smiling)*

(In stumbles Mr. Mediocracy Face. He is late for work and wearing two different socks.) "What's going on? What's everyone talking about?" he says, looking confused.

"I was just making sure that Solid is feeling okay about his big presentation today. He didn't spend a lot of time working on it last night." *(He turns to Solid.)* "What if you answer wrong and the company goes bankrupt?"

(Mr. Mediocracy Face smirks. Then as he sips his coffee, it dribbles down the front of his wrinkled shirt. The stains blend in with the ones that are already there.) "Well, I'm glad I don't have to make presentations. I am perfectly happy sitting at my desk, where it's safe and nobody expects

too much from me," he says. "But I sure wish I could get a promotion and make more money."

(Mr. Perspective Face stands up.) "You always say you wish things could be better, but you seem so happy and content with the way things are. Maybe you should start envisioning what your life could be like and then start making it happen."

(Mr. Mediocracy Face shrugs and laughs. He puts his mug into the sink, leaves it. Then turns and meanders out the door.)

"Wow," said Mr. Negative Face, "Even I get to work on time. That's reminds me. Shouldn't you be early?"

(Solid folds the newspaper and puts it into his briefcase. He walks over to the sink, washes out his coffee mug and puts it away. He turns to leave.)

"Hey, Mr. Negative Face. Have a great day."

And…scene.

Okay, so, this dialogue may have seemed not quite up to the standards of *The Real Show*, because they GO THERE. But, it is an accurate illustration of life in the real, real world. We all know people who are like Mr. Negative Face and Mr. Mediocracy Face. We've talked about them and I have shared a few tools that can help you deal with people who are negative. Notice how Solid does not waste his time arguing or debating with Mr. Negative Face. He is smiling throughout the scene, not because he is smug or clueless. He smiles because he has already filed the negative words into his cerebral spam folder. He cannot waste even a second on negativity, and so he goes on to start his day knowing that he is ready to show up and play.

Mr. Mediocracy Face and Mr. Perspective Face will most likely continue their conversation later over dinner. Because Mr. Perspective Face will want to help, he will share some words of wisdom and hope. As usual, Mr. Medicracy Face will nod like he understands, but will be thinking about playing video games in his room later.

So what's the point of all of this? Just that in our real worlds, the people we live with and work with and are friends with may or may not always have our best interests at heart. Or sometimes, as in the case of my friend who was concerned about my life and time when I announced I was writing this book, may think they are doing what's best for us, but are clueless about who we really are. And that brings me back to getting started DOING.

In this illustration, Mr. Mediocracy Face – in a moment of rare clarity - shares a concern with Mr. Perspective Face. Maybe this is the conversation they have over dinner. He wishes the glass ceiling was not there. Even though the means for him to break through it are clearly in front of him, he still is not motivated enough to change things. He is happy going around in circles and being mediocre.

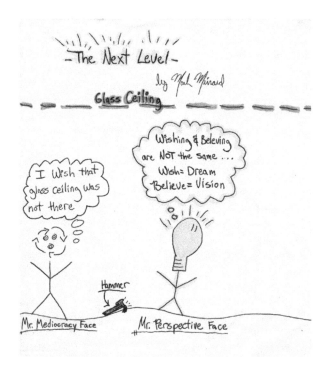

In classic Mr. Perspective Face fashion, he tries to brighten Mr. Mediocracy Face's outlook by giving him a brief lesson on how to take a step toward living his dreams or at least getting to the next level. Both Solid and Mr. Perspective Face know that there is a glass ceiling between every level. In order to move up through the levels, you need to work hard and persevere. You need to file the negative comments and believe in yourself.

But Mr. Mediocracy Face is unable to do any of those things. Of course, Mr. Perspective Face hopes that someday he will, but we all know people like that. And most of them do not change. People who are not willing to overcome the obstacles in their lives for one reason or another find themselves beneath the glass ceiling. And even though the hammer is laying right there in front of them, they are just not motivated enough to pick it up.

But you are reading this book, so I know you are ready. It's time to talk about the next level.

LEVELING UP

"I really believe that challenges shape our perceptions. We can either view them as obstacles that block us from moving where we want to go or directional arrows that point us in the right direction,""
—Dr. Julie Connor

There are so many incredible people out there in the real world who are changing their lives. In our podcast series, Dayne and I get to meet some of them. And will continue to share their stories with the world. But in February 2015, we talked with a woman who figured out how to get to the next level in her life. I want to share some of that interview with you here.

Dr. Julie Connor is the author of *Dreams to Action Trailblazer's Guide*, a book that inspires people to identify and create a plan to achieve their dreams. Julie has inspired many people for more than 30 years to dream big and celebrate their success. We all strive for prosperity and happiness in life, but when it comes to mapping out a strategy to get there, adversity and challenges can sometimes get in the way. In the interview we did with Julie, she talked about how to redirect your thoughts to get to where you want to go.

Julie began the interview by sharing a quote by motivational speaker Brian Tracy: "What you attract into your life is in harmony with your dominant thoughts." Brian was the chief operating officer of a $265 million dollar company before founding his own company, Brian Tracy International. He has written more than 45 books and 300 audio and video programs that help people and companies achieve their goals.[16] Julie shared a challenging time in her life and believes that challenges change us.

"I really believe that challenges shape our perceptions. We can either view them as obstacles that block us from moving where we want to go or directional arrows that point us in the right direction," she said.

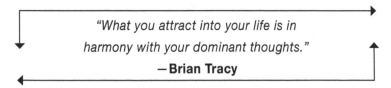

"What you attract into your life is in harmony with your dominant thoughts."
—Brian Tracy

Finding herself without a job, while at the same time earning her doctoral degree, Julie had no idea what to do next. Literally. After a while, she turned to the things she loved most – arts, music, service - and used it to serve others. But Julie had suffered short term memory loss from a traumatic brain injury in a car accident years before. She was struggling and cried out to God. And God told Julie to get out of her comfort zone. As a result, she was called to serve others by providing them with the tools they need to achieve success. She tells people to do three things:

1. Remember what you love.
2. Do what you love.
3. Start somewhere.

Great advice. And if you are interested in hearing more about Julie, check out our podcast, "Failing to the Next Level," at http://www. hipcast.com/podcast/HWZyJb.

Picking up that hammer and breaking through the glass ceiling is an important first step in getting to the next level. Mr. Mediocracy Face believes that the glass ceiling is really preventing him from leveling up and he wishes it wasn't there. Mr. Perception Face sets him straight. He reminds him that wishing is not the same as believing.

Perception makes that big of a difference.

When my wife and I were first dating and we went out in public, we both noticed that people would stare at us. A lot. My wife is a beautiful African-American woman from Sierra Leone, West Africa. I am Caucasian. And we were an interracial couple. Many people stared. Some gave us dirty looks. And some of their looks seemed very judgmental. This made us both very angry, upset, and sad. As I began to sketch Solid and the other characters you meet and come to know in this book (and in future books), I found that Mr. Perspective Face taught us a very important lesson: What you focus on, good or bad, is what you get.

This advice is so simple. It is a simple truth, but is not an easy one to put into practice. It has more to do with changing the way you view the world instead of trying to change the way other people view you, or what you are doing. Well, my wife and I started applying that simple truth. We only focused on the good, and that's what we got.

We got married in 2006, and now when we go out in public, we do not notice the negativity, the stares. Some people still stare at us, but because we changed our perception, we don't notice them. This was a big lesson for me. It led to part two of this simple truth that Mr. Perspective Face taught us: My focus not only attracts good or bad, but it also give out good or bad from me. Because I was focused and dwelling on the way people were staring at us, I fell into the victim's mindset. As a result, I found myself giving off negative vibes toward others. This caused them to give a negative attitude back to me. It created a cycle of negativity. I learned that when my perspective changed it elevated my mindset. With an elevated mindset, I was able to intentionally focus on the positive and not the negative parts of my circumstances. Things really changed for me after that.

I love this quote by former NASA Astronaut James A. Lovell: "The lunar flights give you a correct perception of our existence. You look back at Earth from the moon, and you can put your thumb p to the window and hide the Earth behind your thumb. Everything you've ever known is behind your thumb, and that blue-and-white ball is orbiting a rather normal star, tucked away on the outer edge of a galaxy." Lovell is most famous for commanding the Apollo 13 space mission. He is only one of 24 people to have ever flown to the moon.

Change your mindset and your circumstances will follow.

I promise.

Take a moment now to think about a situation in your life that can change by changing your perception or mindset. Write it here:

_____

_____

_____

What are you going to do change your mindset? Be specific.

_____

_____

_____

Make sure that you are focusing on tangible and concrete examples of what you will do to change your perception. You cannot be like Mr. Mediocracy Face and just dream about something, wishing that it will change. You have to make it change. So the important part of the exercise you just completed is that it doesn't stay on the lines in this book. It is really crucial that you put your plans into action.

Wishing is like dreaming about something to happen. But believing it can actually come true involves create a vision. There is definitely a time and place for wishing and dreaming that something will happen. But that time should be short-lived. The real work and the real changes take place in the next level. That's where your belief kicks in and your vision is realized.

Remember and focus on my two-step business plan:

Stop planning.

Start doing.

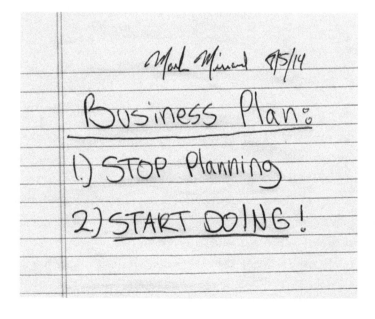

MORE THAN JUST A JOB

"I know it's okay to make mistakes and things don't have to be perfect. It's okay to try and fail. It's the only way to improve and get better."
—**Nate**, *Program Manager at Dreamshine*

Every morning before work, I send out a group text to all of the members of my Dreamshine team. It is a daily devotional/ motivational message that is intended to get everyone fired up and ready for the day. This daily habit has prompted people to send their own quotes around and I can't even begin to tell you how uplifting this is to all of us. Dreamshine has always been and always will be my passion. That's because I know that when I wake up each morning excited and happy to start the day, the people I work with share the same passion as I do.

This is more than just a job.

And like most people in almost all jobs, my team and I have all taken on characteristics of some of my characters in the story of Dreamshine. At one point or another, we have all been Mr. Mediocracy Face, Mr. Perspective Face, and even Mr. Negative Face. But the thing to remember here is that we all have the ability to work things through and to change and become more. We all have the potential to be Mr. Solid Dude.

Let me tell you about Nate.

Nate is the program manager at Dreamshine and has been with us since almost the beginning – more than seven years. Prior to joining the staff at Dreamshine, Nate had worked in the field for more than 10 years. His heart and passion was wonderfully aligned with serving and advocating for individuals with special needs. When he saw that we were established, he was excited about our mission. When Nate came aboard, he brought his talent and heart with him. But before I tell Nate's story, I want to talk about talent and heart.

The development of talent is a life long journey. In order to maximize and accelerate the things you are passionate about and good at, you must develop not only your sense of self, but hone your mindset, as well. Spiritual and political leader, Mahatma Gandhi, once said, "As human beings, our greatness lies not so much in being able to remake the world – that is the myth of the atomic age – as in being able to remake ourselves." This is so true because it inherently says that talent is not enough. Passion is not enough. True success lies in what we do with our passion and our talents. True success lies in learning about ourselves, who we are, what we believe in, and then going from there. In other words, we must be open to developing ourselves and changing our mindsets in order to make the best use of our talents and passion.

"As human beings, our greatness lies not so much in being able to remake the world – that is the myth of the atomic age – as in being able to remake ourselves."
—Mahatma Ghandi

Nate's story is not unusual. However, he was open to change and growth. His ability to look into himself, change and grow was – and still is - extraordinary. Struggling with anxiety and obsessive compulsive issues, Nate came to work for us with great potential. He also started out as Mr. Mediocracy Face. Remember how Mr. Mediocracy Face is his own worst enemy? He is average. Scattered. Not a solid dude. Nate was a true work in progress. In fact, Nate himself would say that he was struggling and had things about himself he knew needed to change. He knew he needed to accept constructive criticism about himself in order to make any changes. He called Dreamshine his catalyst.

Nate recognized something in himself one day while scheduling and setting up an outdoor activity of plastic horseshoes. Because we provide many activities to help people grow and develop socially and physically, horseshoes is an exercise in both. While getting the equipment ready to set up the activity, Nate realized that some of the pieces were missing. He immediately struggled. Nate's mindset was that all of the pieces needed to be there in order for the game to be successful. His obsessiveness was not allowing him to think outside of the box. He couldn't imagine setting up a game unless all of the equipment was there.

I saw that he was having a difficult time and we talked. Nate was struggling with a choice. He could either choose to improvise with the equipment he did have or do nothing at all. I explained to him the why behind what Dreamshine does. I reminded him of the importance of this type of programming for the people we serve with special needs.

Although it may look on the surface like a small thing, Nate's inability to choose to improvise in that moment was big. Choosing to do nothing at all when conditions are not perfect is making the choice to be paralyzed. This paralysis leads to things never getting done and people not living up to their potential. Doing things with what you have, while continually strategizing to make them better, is the best approach to growing and changing.

Now there are thousands of quotes by famous people about self-growth and changing the way you look at things. Gail Sheehy, author of 17 books, including *Passages,* which was published in 1975 and called one of the ten most influential books of our time by the Library of Congress, simply says: "If we don't change, we don't grow. If we don't grow, we aren't really living." After I suggested that he go ahead and play the game, even if he didn't have all of the necessary parts, he was able to change his mindset in that moment. When I told him it was okay to improvise and get creative and that it doesn't have to be perfect, he listened. I told him that he should use his resources and Nate chose not to allow his current mindset – an attitude that dictated to him that things had to be a certain way and there was no way around it – to prevail. We worked together and through true application, Nate was able to change a little and grow. For Nate, this event was a turning point in his career at Dreamshine.

Nate calls the horseshoe incident his defining moment.

Nate believes being able to finally see things from that different mindset is what really got the ball rolling for him. But he will tell you that what keeps the ball rolling is the true leadership of Dreamshine: Me. I have seen transformation in not only Nate, but in the business and other team members. That's because I believe that everyone has the potential to change their mindsets, maximize their talents and use their passion to the highest degree they can. While talking with Nate, I spent a lot of time explaining how this one defining moment could transfer to other challenges he may face in his work or life. We all have many problems we struggle with solving on a day-to-day basis. If we choose to do nothing when conditions are not what we perceive to be perfect, we risk never doing anything at all. Being paralyzed by fear or obsessiveness or anxiety is the worst. In fact, in the Bible, God speaks to fear many times. In fact in Joshua 1:9, God commands us, "Do not be afraid; do not be discouraged, for the LORD your God will be with you wherever you go." God did not make us fearful. We are fearless. And that means not allowing indecision due to fear or obsessiveness or anxiety to paralyze you. You must find a way around the fear and change your mindset in order to grow. At Dreamshine, it is important that everyone on staff strategies to make themselves better. This means not only as leaders at a community where making the lives of people with special needs better is the main purpose and mission, but also as individuals themselves. I cannot stress enough the value of learning and growing.

I am always looking for books, courses and information about leadership for myself, as well as my staff. For example, I participated in a leadership course by Dave Ramsey, who is a personal money management expert, and brought information back to my staff and offered to take anyone interested to a one-day seminar on leadership. Nate is one of my team members who wanted to go…and went. Nate was inspired and motivated by the opportunity. He says that he will remain loyal to Dreamshine and continue doing the best he can do because he feels valued.

"But who wouldn't want to work for a business and an owner that is just this entrepreneurial and eager to bring us up, nurture us to be leaders like himself?" asks Nate.

Nate's experience working at Dreamshine is nothing shy of amazing. He is happy to be a part of what we do. I am happy he is here. Nate has worked hard and knows that it is okay to make mistakes and that things don't have to be perfect. But most of all, Nate knows that it's okay to try and fail. That's the only way to improve and get better.

Nate didn't always feel this way. There were times when he was negative about some of my suggestions and ideas. He was stuck as Mr. Mediocracy Face and stayed in character. But he has come a long way. He digested what we talked about when he was allowing his obsessiveness and anxiety to block his ability to move forward while setting up a game of horseshoes. He took time to think about it all and with a bit of trial and error, has able to get past it. Learning that it's okay to make mistakes, as long as you are not too fearful to make them, is a positive thing. Remember...being paralyzed and taking no action because things aren't perfect is not okay. Nate had great potential in the years he didn't work at Dreamshine. Once he got here and his talents were recognized and nurtured, he grew. He has developed the leadership skills that were always there. He has become less and less like Mr. Mediocracy Face and more and more like Solid.

Seeing the strengths in other people is so important. For me, seeing Nate's positive and strong qualities, talents, and passion enabled me to help him move forward. This not only benefits Nate, but it benefits the participants at Dreamshine, as well as the entire team, business, and me. It's a win-win situation all around.

Now I want you to think about a job where your talents and strengths were ignored. Your ideas were not heard. Your passion was discounted. Close your eyes, take a few moments and think about how that made you feel. Write it here:

_____

_____

_____

Now think about a time in your life – or while at a job – when someone recognized something in you. A strength. A talent. A passion. Whatever. Think about what happened and how you felt when that part of you was seen, nurtured, and developed. Close your eyes and take a moment to focus on that. Jot down how that made you feel:

_____

_____

_____

It's no surprise that being recognized for your strengths and talents feels better. Like Nate, we all grow when given the right support in the right way. Nate's passion and talents are valued at Dreamshine, and as a result, he feels motivated to do the very best he can do every single day he comes to work.

> *"Being paralyzed and taking no action because things aren't perfect is not okay."*

To do the best with what you have and continually strategize to be better is the best approach. You must have the faith to move mountains. You must push yourself above the Mr. Mediocracy Face's mindset and abolish fear, adversity and negativity. Every day at work I see how this can play out. I see passion and talent and the potential for strong leaders. Working at a place like this is empowering not only for the staff, but for me, as well. It is a privilege to use what I have learned to help other people change their mindsets, harness their talents and use their passion for the greater good.

Working at Dreamshine has made me a Solid Dude.

Look at this illustration. Solid is holding up his mountain of fear, adversity and negativity. He has the faith to move that mountain to rise about the land of mediocraty. He has the ability and the tools to step out of mediocre and into the life he wants. He stands his ground and the fear of the unknown melts away. He always keeps his eye on his dream. He is focused on and follows the light. And for me - and I hope you, too - that means pushing through no matter what. It means finding the strengths and good in others so that they can learn to move mountains, too. It means knowing that your WHY is what propels you to do what you have to do.

By now you know that my WHY of Dreamshine is to give each individual the opportunity to be treated with respect and dignity. It is to provide a nurturing and supportive environment where adults with special needs can strengthen their educational and social skills and even earn a paycheck. It is to give all participants the chance to be productive and social and to shine. If I have to change or adapt, develop a new set of tools, or improvise and make mistakes, then so be it. Learning and changing and growing is what it's all about and why we are here.

BRIAN'S STORY

"Mark rocked the boat."
—**Tammy**, *parent*

Brian was the first participant to come to Dreamshine. I met him a year before while working with him on the weekends. Brian's mother, Tammy, and I talked a lot about my dream. She liked what she heard. At the time, she was looking for a placement for Brian during the day and promised that if I opened Dreamshine, she would sign him up to attend.

Brian is an energetic and loving young man in his twenties with special needs. Before he came to Dreamshine, he started out at the county workshop. This is the same place I talked about at the beginning of the book. Tammy calls the industrial setting of the workshop "a warehouse with tables." Because Tammy is a hands-on and involved parent, she would pop in regularly to see how Brian was doing while he was there. What she saw was both disheartening and sad. She describes Brian's day as repetitive and lonely. On one visit, when she dropped into the county workshop, she said she saw Brian sitting alone at a table flipping through magazines with his hand on his head. The only other option for him was to place stickers on the back of wallpaper over and over and over again.

Brian stayed at the county workshop for two weeks before Tammy had to get him out of there. "Brian deserved more. I wanted more for him," she said.

Tammy worked from home and kept Brian home with her for two years. Then she secured funding to send him to another home placement. Brian tried out his new program, but did not want to go back. When I opened Dreamshine, Tammy had many challenges and obstacles to overcome to get Brian through our doors, but she was successful. As a result, Brian spends his days socializing, being challenged, loved, and valued. In fact, when Friday rolls around, Brian gets upset because he can't come back until Monday.

Tammy says that as a parent, Dreamshine is an answer from God. She has told me that she was sure she would never be able to find a nurturing and supportive program for her son. Can you imagine how disheartening that must be? Tammy's desire for happiness and value for her son triggered my why. Brian was my first participant, but my why is not only focused on the people who attend my program. My why is also to empower families. As I kicked down doors to get Brian into – and keep him in – Dreamshine, I have had to be persistent and focused. Throughout the process, I have had to teach Tammy how to be persistent and focused, too.

"I always say God didn't give me Brian if He wasn't going to give me the means to take care of him," Tammy said. "And He has put people in my life that I feel like I didn't deserve. But Brian did."

At Dreamshine, Brain has choices. He develops his social skills, gets plenty of exercise and is happy. More importantly, though, Tammy sees how much the staff teach and love her son. Brian gets so much out of Dreamshine, but we get so much out of Brian, too.

It's a two-way street.

Brian loves Dreamshine. Tammy says he looks forward to going every morning and doesn't like coming home at 3 o'clock. She knows he feels needed and a part of something. That's because every day Brian gets to socialize and be appreciated for who he is. He communicates and laughs. He works and plays.

And he gets to fish.

DREAMSHINE: MY 1,000-MILE JOURNEY

➤ ← ➤ ←

*"I used to think God guided us by opening
and closing doors, but now I know sometimes
God wants us to kick some doors down."*
—**Bob Goff**, author of *Love Does*

E veryone at Dreamshine gets to fish. But it wasn't always that way. After we moved to our 2.5-acre property with the log home and pond, we did not have the necessary funds to construct a building that could accommodate bigger electric wheelchairs. By this time, many individuals with different types of special needs were attending our program. They were thrilled to have a place like Dreamshine to come to. But we were limited in space and ultimately knew we needed another building. We wanted to make sure we had an appropriate space to provide all of the exciting and stimulating programs we envisioned. We visualized a building with an open floor plan that was fully wheelchair-accessible. We pictured a roomy building that overlooked our pond that everyone could enjoy. This vision for our Waterfront Lodge became an important focus and piece in the puzzle of our growing company.

I began scouring magazines and cutting out photographs of different styles of buildings we liked. I printed pictures of our pond and pasted them onto a poster board along with photos of the building styles I had found. I also posted inspirational quotes, as well. One of my favorites is by author and speaker, Bob Goff. He said, "I used to think God guided us by opening and closing doors, but now I know sometimes God wants us to kick some doors down."

Bob Goff is the author of *Love Does: Discovering a Secretly Incredible Life in an Ordinary World,* a book about DOING. In 2003, as an attorney, Goff founded a non-profit human rights organization called Restore International, an international group whose goal is to "try to change a few lives for the better" in India and Uganda.[17] In his book, *Love Does,* Goff shares the chapters of his life and how each story comes together to prove that with love, faith, and the right attitude, anyone can be inspired. In his book, Goff writes: "Failure is just part of the process, and it's not just okay; it's better than okay. God doesn't want failure to shut us down. God didn't make it a three-strikes-and-you're-out sort of thing. It's more about how God helps us dust ourselves off so we can swing for the fences again. And all of this without keeping a meticulous record of our screw-ups."[18]

Wow.

Not being afraid of failing is one of the keys to success. That includes not being afraid of being terrible. Because I am not afraid of being terrible and because I have great faith that I am spending my life in the way God wants me to, I will be successful, even if and when I fail. That's the way we learn to be better.

Bob Goff is a lot like Solid. His faith and love have gotten him far in life. The attitude he displays as he travels around, speaking and motivating others to do the same, is exactly what Solid would do. Solid knows that having a vision and making sure that it is manifested equals success. Getting to the top of that mountain - to the 1,000th mile – means never giving in, never giving up.

Kind of like my Waterfront Lodge story.

I cut out photographs, put up a motivational poster board, began sharing my vision of this new building with my team and we began to take action. My sister and I went to one bank. Then we went to another bank. Then another. And another. We were received enthusiastically and the loan officers were excited about giving us a loan for our project. We spent months providing financial statements and every piece of personal information you can imagine. We spent hundreds of hours collecting everything they needed, meeting with them, and running around in circles. Ultimately, not one of the banks came through with a loan for us. Each one had a different answer as to why we had been denied. And because not one of them gave us any constructive feedback, we were unable do things differently and move forward.

We pushed on, though.

After nine months of more banks, more meetings, more running around in circles collecting and surrendering financial information, we were right back where we started. No bank would give us a loan. We were discouraged, but not broken. We continued to share our vision of the new building and even had architectural drawings made. We held a presentation for the families of the individuals who attended Dreamshine at the time and told them that the building would be ready by Fall. This created much excitement and generated a waiting list of individuals who anticipated starting the program in September.

Before we knew it, it was August and, after working with another bank for three months, we had been rejected again. They assured us they could help. They told us the loan and our dreams for a new building would happen. But in the end, they turned us down. My sister and I had so many people counting on us. There were now two weeks left before new participants were signed up to start.

I was terrified, angry, and heartbroken. How could I tell these families that I could not deliver on my promise? How could I let all of these people down? They were counting on me. People I knew began telling me that it was okay. They said I had done all that I could do and should give up. They told me to drop Plan A and think about a Plan B. They said that the Waterfront Lodge was not meant to be.

This illustration, like the one of Solid above, is a piece of a bigger picture. The people who told me to quit and find my Plan B are like Mr. Mediocracy Face. Here he says, "You are all the way back to mile 400. It's easier to just give up and go back to the Land of Mediocracy."

If I had listened and stopped trying, I would have stalled out even before I got half way through my 1,000-mile journey. I would have stopped at mile 400 and settled for whatever was the easier.

I would have become Mr. Mediocracy Face.

As I heard what people were saying about giving up, I knew in my heart I could not. I put on my sneakers and sweats and jogged to clear my head. As I ran, I argued with God. I cried out, "Why? Why? Why?" On that run, I agonized over and prayed about what I would tell the families of the participants who were so excited about attending Dreamshine, Then God spoke to me. He told me that I would not be telling those families anything. God made it clear to me that I was going to build that building.

Because of my faith and my close walk with God, I knew that He had communicated with me. He did not tell me how I would get there, but he confirmed His will for my life. In that moment when I heard God's voice in my heart, I was reminded of my WHY. I was reminded that the reason for Dreamshine and everything I had done up until that point was for Him. My Why started with God. Within minutes, I was armed and ready. I repeated the first part of Isaiah 54:17, "…no weapon that is fashioned against you shall succeed." [19] I said that verse out loud again and again. I knew in my heart that I would succeed at figuring out how to get our building.

I would succeed.

It takes courage to manifest great change. It takes bravery to be like Christ and to not conform. For Jesus, this means not conforming to the norm. You have to be a little insane. A little bit of insanity mixed with incredible faith equals the entrepreneur. It is the successful entrepreneur – or any person striving toward a vision - who makes it over the 400-mile setback and goes all the way to the 1,000th mile. The important take-away here is that it's all about God.

> *A little bit of insanity mixed with*
> *incredible faith equals the entrepreneur.*

Since Christ is in my heart, my vision and dream for the Waterfront Lodge started with Him. Already familiar with what this felt like, because the original vision of Dreamshine was put in my heart by God, I was led to proceed using my heart as my guide. Using my heart to guide me, however, never means that I do not use my brain. That would be ridiculous. It just means that my journey – my 1,000-mile journey – is guided by my heart.

Here's another piece of the big picture.

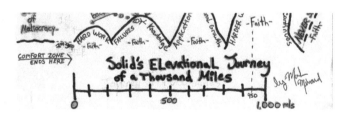

Look closely at this illustration and you will see that faith is present at mile 0. It is there at mile 400. It is there at mile 950. And it is there at the 1,000th mile. Without faith, this journey would not be possible. Without faith, this journey would begin and end in the Land of Mediocracy. Without my great faith, I would not have left my comfort zone. I would not have fought the many battles and dealt with the seemingly impossible odds and challenges to open Dreamshine. Without that faith, the participants and their families, my own family and my staff would not be benefitting from this incredible adventure/

business I've created. By applying the principles you see in the picture – faith, hard work, failure, knowledge, application, personal growth, even harder work, and never settling – the dream and vision of Dreamshine that God gave me years ago has been realized.

THE WATERFRONT LODGE, FINALLY.

→ ← → ←

"If you can't fly, then run.
If you can't run, then walk.
If you can't walk, then crawl.
But whatever you do, you have to
keep moving forward."
—Martin Luther King, Jr.

D reamshine is and always will be my first 1,000-mile journey. It was and is my vision. It was what God put on my heart. It is what God continuously puts on my heart. And so, I regrouped and forged ahead. We immediately went back to DOING. We took ACTION. Before long, we had a temporary wheelchair-accessible mobile home delivered. We decorated it and made it look awesome and homey. This allowed our new participants to start on time, but everyone knew it was not a permanent solution. We let everyone know that construction for the new lodge had been pushed back and we assured them that by November the new building will be built and ready.

But we still did not have a loan.

Then I had an idea. I decided to think outside of the box and focus on other sources of financial help. Who said you need a bank to get a loan? I knew that commercial interest rates were way higher than the interest rates people were collecting who had money sitting in a savings or money market account. I recognized Dreamshine for the business opportunity that it was. My business could be a way for people to make a solid investment with a high return. Working overtime and as hard as we could, we were able to secure three different investors. We also decided to change the building plans. Instead of a two-story structure, we were going to build a one-story lodge. Making this decision would cut costs by about 40 percent and double the size of the main floor. This also allowed us to add the now-famous, all-accessible covered porch which overhangs the pond. But even after these alterations to the building plans and with three investors, we were still short by about $35,000.

Then I had another out-of-the-box idea. I approached the project's builder and asked if he would consider a short-term investment. We asked if he would give us an 18-month loan at the commercial interest rates. The up sides for him were that he would not only end up making more money, but the payback time was quick. He had never been asked to do anything like this before as a builder, but after going over the numbers and seeing the monthly payment schedule I had prepared, he agreed. They broke ground the next day and we had our grand opening of the Waterfront Lodge on November 12, 2013.

Now, some might say that the changes we made to our plans and the way we went after funding was our Plan B. All along, however, I knew in my heart that there was never any Plan B. There was no other option for us other than our Plan A. What we did to make our lodge a reality makes me think of the adversity Jesus faced. Jesus was crucified in order to reach His vision: to be resurrected , forgive all of our sins, and conquer the impossible – death. But what if Jesus gave up? I think we all know the answer to that question. Christ chose to show us the importance of not giving up on your vision.

Jesus walked the walk.

He showed us there is power in never giving up. He proved that it takes the impossible in order for miracles to happen.

Going through everything we went through to get our Waterfront Lodge funded and built taught me many things. It taught me about faith. It taught me how to dare to believe that nothing is impossible. It taught me that miracle territory is not found within our comfort zones.

My good man, Dan Miller, author of *48 Days to The Work You Love,* says, "When you have nothing, anything is possible." This is what it is all about: putting Faith into Action and ensuring your why is bigger than your fear. And this is how God shows His amazing glory through these impossible circumstances. Jesus looked up at them and said, "With man this is impossible, but with God all things are possible." (Matthew 19:26).

Now let's go back and pull all of the pieces of this puzzle together. Let's take a look at the bigger picture. On the next page, you will see how the illustrations of Mr. Mediocracy Face, Mr. Perspective Face, and Solid fit together. Look carefully at the picture I drew. Analyze what you see happening.

Notice that:

1. The first step begins where the comfort zone ends.
2. Faith is intertwined throughout the entire 1,000-mile journey.
3. Work hard and then harder will get you over the hills and mountains of adversity.

4. The impossible is within reach if you see failures as a way to gain knowledge.

5. The application of all you learn is the only way to personal growth.

6. You might get knocked back to mile 400, but you are not out of the game.

7. Solid never settles.

8. This journey is just the beginning.

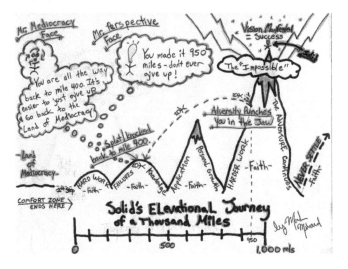

I encourage you now to go back and makes notes in the margin and on the illustration. Circle things that you are already doing. Underline things that you need to work on. In fact, I would recommend that you make a copy of page 92 and really think about what you can be doing to reach your vision. What do you need to do to stand where Solid is standing? Tape the illustration in places where you can see it. Spend a few minutes every day looking it over and taking it in. Everything you need to succeed is in that illustration. All you have to do is learn to use what's there.

Right now, take a moment and write a few lines about your impressions of my illustration and what it means to you.

_____

_____

_____

_____

_____

_____

Great. As we move forward and you continue reading, I want to help you see your vision manifested. I want to give you tools that will help you succeed in whatever it is you want to do. Each time you complete a 1,000-mile journey, you equip yourself for the next journey. And the next. And the next. Opening Dreamshine was my first 1,000 miles. When it came time to plan and build the Waterfront Lodge, I was more experienced and more knowledgeable. I was in a better position and able to forge through the adversity to focus on achieve Plan A. My foundation had been built and I was more trained and carried better equipment with me. I was ready to climb mountains of higher altitudes. And like Solid, I did.

WHAT IT TAKES

"I do not make excuses, I make changes.
I do not make compromises, only improvises."
—Mark Minard

A t the beginning of this book, I shared a story about how reading changed my life. It still does. But reading is not the only thing that helps me overcome challenges, motivates me, and clears my head. After jail, after I hit my rock bottom, and at the same time I began reading that first life-altering book, I also began to exercise, lift weights, and jog. The more I jog, the more I appreciate its meditative qualities and how beneficial it is to clearing my head.

I think best when I am moving. When I'm on a serious phone call, I can be seen pacing around inside my house. More often, though, I can be found walking around the outside of my house in giant laps while talking. To the "average" mindset, it may seem insane or crazy, but for me, moving gets my blood flowing. When my blood is flowing, I can focus and engage. I have learned that in order to have clarity of thought, I must first clear my head. So while there are times when a good book by a motivational author or an inspirational video on YouTube will do the trick, when I have something important to work out or work through, a good jog or a long walk is what I need.

In the event you are more of a book or video type of person, here are some of my all-time favorites.

Mark's Top Ten Motivating Authors and Speakers (in no particular order):

1. *Walt Disney*
2. *Albert Einstein*
3. *Nelson Mandela*
4. *Jesus Christ*
5. *Jesus' Disciples*
6. *Eric Thomas*
7. *Martin Luther King, Jr.*
8. *Bob Goff*
9. *Dave Ramsey*
10. *Bishop T.D. Jakes*

Hey, we are all busy. I have five children, a company, I am writing this book, I started a podcast, I am coaching, and booking speaking events. It is imperative that I create the time I need for clarity. As a child, I was labeled with Attention Deficit Hyperactivity Disorder, or ADHD. As an adult, I claim my ADHD as a gift from God. I do not make excuses, I make changes. I do not make compromises, only improvises.

Through the challenges, struggles, joys, and tears of opening and running Dreamshine, I have learned so many things. Taking a leadership role in a business that operates on such a human level means that many things change all the time. State rules and regulations are revised. Funding guidelines change. Even the people I motivate and who motivate me every day change. This is life. Struggles and challenges are ever-present. Each step forward through the tough times has made me stronger. In kicking down a few doors, I got to see my vision manifest itself. It hasn't been easy, but it sure has been worth it.

It takes a lot to be a great leader.

Real leadership is about getting to know each personality on your team. It's not enough to care for the welfare and well-being of the people you are leading. You have to go one step further. I have learned that it takes more than thinking. It takes action. People cannot read my mind, and I cannot read theirs. But there is something to that old saying about how our actions speak louder than words. For me and my team at Dreamshine, what we do on a daily basis is so personal and important to each individual who comes to our program that anything less than our best is not acceptable. That means how we conduct ourselves with our clients, and how we conduct ourselves with each other. A true leader leads in the way he wants his team to act. In other words, if I want my team members to be respectful of each other and the people we serve, then I had better be respectful.

Leadership expert John C. Maxwell says, "A leader is one who knows the way, goes the way, and shows the way."

Amen.

I used to think that everyone could read my mind. I used to think that my team members knew how much I appreciated them. But I have learned this is not true. I have learned that I must be intentional, even if it means clearing time on my calendar to make sure people know how much I appreciate them. Now, when someone at Dreamshine goes above and beyond or is caught being awesome, I make sure they know it. In fact, at Dreamshine, we give out tokens of awesomeness. These tokens allow the person being rewarded to play a miniature claw grabbing game filled with $10 and $20 bills.

Really.

Maybe you're thinking right now that putting reminders on my calendar to help me remember to thank the people on my team for the awesome things they do is a sign that I don't care. But it really is the opposite. I am so busy and the reminder forces me to not forget. The reminders on my calendar to thank and encourage is my intentional way of showing gratitude. This is a huge thing because it develops a mindset within the leaders on our teams. Saying "you are doing a great job" is the norm and becomes a part of our organization's culture. This mindset does not only apply to work environments. Making a point to proactively acknowledge someone's contributions works in all areas of our lives. You can be grateful for someone and make sure they know it if you are a business owner, teacher, coach, parent, or spouse. This works in all relationships and interactions you have. And by making the effort to show appreciation, you are leading by serving.

A strong leader is intentional and makes sure the behaviors of all not only benefit the whole team, but are aligned with the company's principles and core values. At Dreamshine, our mission is to ensure the highest quality of independence, personal growth, and social interactions for individuals with special needs. That's a tall order. My leadership skills have had to grow and change in order to make sure we meet that high standard every single day. Finding ways to encourage and reward team members who are meeting that mission is one of my favorite things to do.

Not too long ago, one of my "dream team" members hit his fifth anniversary working with us. At our monthly Dream Team meeting, we honored his accomplishments with a speech. Then the team, all 14 of us, gave him a standing ovation. After the awesome round of applause, I gave him a box. Two weeks before the meeting, I made it my business to find out what he really wanted. I learned this team member was an avid comic book and toy collector. He has many action figures proudly displayed in his home in glass cases. His collection is really cool and worth a lot of money. As I dug a little deeper, I discovered that he always wanted a specific Indiana Jones collector's edition action figure. It was hard to find and it was expensive, but worth it to see his expression when he opened the box I gave him.

This is what I'm talking about.

Great leadership searches for, rewards and encourages behavior that aligns with your organization's principles and values. Being a serving leader means making sure everyone on the team contributes in a positive way. Stephen Covey, author of *The Seven Habits of Highly Effective People,* and other books, is a sought after educator, businessman, and speaker. Covey has built a reputation that is based on his beliefs about becoming proactive and intentional. For example, a few of his seven habits include being proactive, always keeping the end in mind, and working toward understanding first. Covey says that "you have to decide what your highest priorities are and have the courage – pleasantly, smilingly, unapologetically, to say 'no' to other things. And the way you do that is by having a bigger 'yes' burning inside."[20]

> *"Moral authority comes from following universal and timeless principles like honesty, integrity, treating people with respect."*
> —**Stephen Covey**

At Dreamshine, our WHY is that bigger yes. As the leader, it is my responsibility to keep my eye on our WHY. It is my duty to the individuals who have come to rely on our programs to make sure every single team member is on board and creates an environment that screams our WHY. Covey says that "Moral authority comes from following universal and timeless principles like honesty, integrity, treating people with respect." I believe it is my moral responsibility and authority to make sure our vision is lived out every day. I get to do really cool things, like giving awesome gifts to team leaders who are deserving, but that also means I have to do the hard things.

Being a leader means always keeping your eye on the ball.

FEELINGS VS. PRINCIPLES: PART ONE

"The main thing is to keep the main thing the main thing."
—**Stephen Covey**, author, educator, speaker

t takes great courage to be an effective leader. I learned this firsthand as I was growing Dreamshine. In order to create a nurturing, safe, educational, and stimulating environment where individuals with special needs feel loved, safe, and challenged, it was imperative that I cling to the set of principles that guide me. As my company grew, I became more excited about leadership. I realized through trial and error that being a good leader means reframing from making excuses. It means embracing accountability. It means being transparent.

So what does that look like?

My family attends a great church. The pastor is committed and smart and I admire him. Not too long ago, he shared his struggles publicly with our church family. He opened up about his feelings about religion and how he felt. He stood before us and admitted to being just like the rest of us. He talked about the issues that were challenging him at the time and spoke frankly and earnestly. By having the courage to stand before us and admit that he was conflicted and struggling made him transparent. It made him vulnerable and real.

It made me respect him even more than I already had.

Becoming real to the people you lead is the definition of true leadership. Without transparency, leadership is not true at all. It is leading without integrity. Leading without integrity means leading without truth. It means leading without example and goes against what I just said a little while ago about how actions are important when it comes to leadership.

Being a good leader means reframing from making excuses. It means embracing accountability. It means being transparent.

Think about a strong and positive relationship you are involved in right now. Think about the dynamics between you and the other person in the relationship. Maybe you are a parent of a teenager, or a small child. Maybe you are a newlywed or someone who has been married for many years. Maybe you have a best friend that you've known since grade school. Maybe you just met someone new. Take a moment and think about what makes that relationship strong. What draws you to that person and allows you to be yourself and open up about anything? Why is that person in your life in the first place? Write the top three characteristics of that relationship here:

_____

_____

_____

Good job.

Now let's think about differences. How do the differences play out in your relationship? Do those differences matter? Spend a few moments thinking about the ways you and the other person in your friendship/ marriage/family/work environment are not alike. Write a few sentences about how you are not similar and whether or not it makes a difference. Maybe it even makes your relationship stronger.

_____

_____

_____

_____

Great.

According to Alan Loy McGinnis, minister and author of many self-help books, "People with deep and lasting friendships may be introverts, extroverts, young, old, dull, intelligent, homely, good-looking, but the one characteristic they all have in common is openness." In the same article, "Developing Friendships That Last," writer Sheryl DeWitt xsays that true friends are loving, trustworthy, open, and respectful. She also says that a true friend is a servant, a speaker of truth, and a positive person.[21] In my own life, I have found this to be true. In my marriage, as a parent, as a friend, as a business owner, all of the characteristics listed above are very important in building and keeping relationships – whether they are personal or work-related.

In America, we have a love-hate relationship with celebrities. Whether we want to admit it or not, we are elated when someone wins an Emmy or Grammy award, and we are crushed when they are caught being untrue or deceptive. These are people we don't even know, but because of their public accomplishments, we feel connected to them in some way. We cheer them on. We look up to them. We call them our role models. For example, you don't have to be a baseball fan – or to be more specific, a fan of the Pittsburgh Pirates or San Francisco Giants – to know about what happened to Barry Bonds. It was all over the news. One season he is gaining on and breaking Major League Baseball hitting and home run records, and the next season he is indicted on charges for perjury and the obstruction of justice because he allegedly lied to a grand jury about steroid use. And whether or not he was guilty of anything, in my mind, he lost points. And not just with me. Bonds is still waiting to be elected into the National Baseball Hall of Fame. I think he would have gotten in if he had done one simple thing: told the truth.

When you are in the public eye, telling the truth is not an easy thing to do. So much is at stake. So many people might turn their backs and cheer for someone else. But let me tell you something: Telling the truth is not easy for most of us to do. Telling the truth means:

- Sharing your struggles
- No more excuses
- Being accountable for your actions
- Showing your humanness
- Owning up to your mistakes
- Saying, "I'm sorry."

Telling the truth means we might have been wrong. It means maybe we misjudged someone or spoke too soon. It might even mean that maybe we didn't tell the whole truth, or even just part of the truth. Telling the truth may mean making yourself more vulnerable than you are comfortable being. But - and believe me when I say this - it is important for all of us to admit failures and stop making excuses. And it is especially important for leaders to tell the truth.

So let's examine why people make excuses and have such a hard time admitting their mistakes and failures.

In an interesting excerpt from a 2007 National Public Radio, or NPR, podcast entitled, "Why It's Hard to Admit to Being Wrong," social psychologist Elliot Aronson says "our brains work hard to make us think we are doing the right thing, even in the face of sometimes overwhelming evidence to the contrary." In the book he co-authored with Carol Tavris, *Mistakes Were Made (But Not By Me)*, Aronson says that hardly anyone ever says, "I blew it!" He uses the example of doomsday predictions and the people behind them. When these true believers, who are convinced that the world will end on a predicted day and time, are proved wrong and the world keeps on going, rarely do they admit that their prediction was wrong. In fact, many of those doomsday predictors go on to become even more convinced that they have powers to make these kinds of predictions.[22] Let's use an event that occurred more than 50 years ago and a prediction made by someone called Marian Keech.

Marian Keech is the alias given to a Chicago housewife who prophesized that the world would end on December 21, 1954 because of an enormous and devastating flood. She had a group of believers and many of them quit their jobs, left college, walked out on their spouses, and gave away their homes and worldly possessions in order to be ready to be picked up by a flying saucer. The group believed that the spacecraft would rescue them before the world ended on the 21st. They sat around at Keech's home praying and waiting for the flying saucer, which of course never arrived. In fact, by 4 a.m. when Keech realized they would not be rescued from disaster, she began crying. But just 45 minutes later, Keech turned things around. Instead of admitting that she may have been wrong about the end of the world, Marian Keech convinced her followers – well, those who stuck around – that it was their prayers and devotion that saved humanity and the Earth from the flood that would destroy it. They had saved the world from destruction. From there, the group – which had always purposely kept the media at arm's length - sought out interviews and called the newspapers to report that they were the reason everyone else was alive.

You can't make this stuff up.

And I didn't. Marian Keech's story was documented in a book written in 1964 entitled *When Prophecy Fails: A Social and Psychological Study of a Modern Group That Predicted the Destruction of the World.* The authors, Leon Festinger, Henry Reicken, and Stanly Schachter documented Keech's UFO religion group and documented the consequences when predictions and expectations go wrong. This reportedly was the first published case study in social psychology of its kind.[23]

Aronson and Tavris also talk about Keech and her religious group in their book about why it's hard to admit mistakes. They quote Festinger's book and call it cognitive dissonance, which according to Dictionary. com is "anxiety that results from simultaneously holding contradictory or otherwise incompatible attitudes, beliefs, or the like, as when one likes a person but disapproves strongly of one of his or her habits."

So, what's my point?

Not opening up and admitting that you may have been wrong, or untrue, or used performance-enhancing drugs to win a baseball game/ bike race/wrestling match/swim meet tarnished your reputation. It sends the people who look up to or at you conflicting messages. A real-life example of cognitive dissonance could be: I love baseball and work really hard to be good at it, but I take steroids to make me a better hitter.

It's true if you believe it's true.

So when I said that my pastor opened up to us and admitted that he struggled with the same issues that we struggle with, he became someone who was human and respected. He earned respect by admitting he wasn't perfect and that made him a better church leader.

FORTITUDE is:

BRAVERY

BOLDNESS

COURAGE

GRIT

SPUNK

TENACITY

PERSEVERANCE

HEART

PITH

WHAT IT TAKES

GUTSINESS

STRENGTH

FEARLESSNESS

VALOR

BACKBONE

—from Thesaurus.com

That's my point.

To be a great leader means you have to stick to your principles at all times. You need to admit failures. You need to say, "I made that mistake. I am sorry. I will work on it. I have learned from it." This is the way to gain the respect of your team and the people in your life that you share meaningful relationships with. I found this great article on Forbes. com written by blogger and contributor Amy Rees Anderson. In her online article, "Admitting You Were Wrong Doesn't Make You Weak - It Makes You Awesome!" Anderson defines fortitude as the umbrella term for admitting mistakes and saying "I'm sorry." She even uses the word *Boo-yah* to describe what she thinks of fortitude.

"If we want to be genuinely successful in both business and life, we have to be willing to set aside our pride, our fears, and our insecurities, and really come to recognize that to be a true leader that is deserving of their position of authority, we must earn – not demand – the respect of our coworkers. The journey toward earning their respect begins the moment we recognize our mistakes and have the integrity and fortitude to utter the words, 'I was wrong, and I am sorry.'"

—Amy Rees Anderson

"I don't know exactly why so many in the world carry that false belief that admitting their mistakes makes them weak," writes Anderson, "but I can tell you how I learned to recognize that the opposite was true." In the article, she tells the story of a disagreement between a father and his teenage daughter. Anderson was in her twenties at the time and this family were friends of hers. She listened carefully and deemed the dad to be correct in what he was telling his daughter, but at the same time, she was shocked because he wasn't saying it in a positive way. As a leader of their family, he was expressing himself in a demeaning and hurtful tone. Anderson wrestled with whether or not to point that out, but was saved from having to make that decision when she happened to overhear the dad telling his daughter he was wrong and that he was sorry. The reason Anderson shares this seemingly insignificant exchange is because she says it was the first time she had ever seen someone in authority apologize in that manner. Then once it was all over, she admits his behavior changed her life.

"Seeing his behavior that day," Anderson writes, "changed my life, because I was able to recognize that the reason I now saw him as a leader of great fortitude was his willingness to honestly and humbly admit his mistake, especially to someone subordinate to him." [24]

Anderson's insight fits right in with my belief that we gain respect by being open and honest and human. I've said this already, but it is important enough to say again now: Character growth is an ongoing thing and something that we all must be intentional about. Putting principles into action takes practice and courage.

It takes fortitude.

I have learned that this is difficult for me to do and something I intentionally have to work at. I have learned to stay laser-focused on my principles and values.

This is something Solid knows a lot about.

FEELINGS VS. PRINCIPLES: PART TWO

> *"It takes great courage to be an effective leader,*
> *and it starts with principles."*
> **—Mark Minard**

As a serving leader, I often ask myself, "What do I stand for?" This question gets at the root of my WHY. It helps me tackle the tough issues that come up at work, at home, and out in the world. People look at conflict as a negative thing, but if you are working together with someone and are on the same team, same page, and are coming into it with respect for one another, resolution can be reached.

Like admitting you are wrong, reaching a respectful resolution is another thing that takes practice and courage. I have learned that even though conflict is not fun or easy to deal with, tackling tough issues can help both parties involved. In fact, I learned that things often get worse if conflict is avoided.

Here's a real example of what I mean:

Awhile back, I had a situation at Dreamshine where I was avoiding problems and unable to have a hard conversation with one of my team members. This person's behavior was not aligned with our principles and I soon realized that by avoiding the tough conversation, I was enabling the negative behavior (another thing that did not align with my own principles.) When I recognized that the behavior of this one team member was not in line with Dreamshine's principles, I also saw that it was affecting the entire team. Because I could not bring myself to deal with the situation, I was not serving my team. This went on for almost two years. This situation that I put off dealing with caused me to lose some valuable people. Because of this one person's behavior, good, strong and principled employees were quitting. It took me a while to learn that in order to get resolution, I needed to separate the value this person had with the behavior being exhibited. When I finally had the hard conversation, I made it clear that the negative attitude and behavior could no longer be at Dreamshine. I told my team member that he was welcome, but the attitude and behavior must change. The behavior and attitude that did not align with our core principles and values were no longer welcome.

This experience was difficult for me, but I learned so much from it. I did let that person stay on and things were better for a while. But once the negative behaviors and attitude resurfaced, I made the decision to let him go. That was the right thing to do. Yes it was difficult. Yes it was not the way I wanted things to go. But, once that team member left, the rest of the team unified.

Bottom line: I learned that if people are not willing to grow, it is a disservice to the rest of the team to allow that person to get away with that.

Going through that difficult experience made me realize that principles matter. It also taught me that it takes practice and courage to ensure that those principles are respected and realized. Having to fire someone who was not living up to Dreamshine's principles was one of the toughest things I've had to do. But it was necessary. Principles are that important. Never turn your back on your principles. It's that important and it's that difficult. To quote my mentor Eric Thomas, "If it was easy, everyone would do it."

The good news is that facing mistakes head on gets easier. It's never pleasant, but not facing difficult situations is worse. Being a good leader is challenging. All good leaders face defining moments like the one I faced. That fork in the road where we have to decide whether to confront or ignore issues forces us to really think about and decide what's important.

Can you think of a situation in life where you had to confront an issue or situation or person head on? Try to remember how hard that was to do. What did you think about or do to prepare yourself to face that person or tough situation? Think for another few minutes and write about it here.

_____

_____

_____

_____

It is common knowledge that athletes prepare themselves mentally before a big game. In fact, researchers have found that many coaches and athletes believe that being able to "reach optimal sport performance is 90 percent mental." Those same researchers studied athletes and coaches and believed that the formula for "optimal sport performance" is concentration and motivation.[25]

I get that.

So does Ken Dryden, former goalie for the Montreal Canadians. In his quote about ice hockey and being prepared mentally for a game, Dryden talks about the importance of concentration and mental fortitude. Dryden says, "Because the demands on a goalie are mostly mental, it means that for a goalie, the biggest enemy is himself. Not a puck, not an opponent, not a quirk of size or style. Him. The stress and anxiety he feels when he plays…[is] in constant ebb and flow, but never disappearing. The successful goalie understands these neuroses, accepts them, and puts them under control. The unsuccessful goalie is distracted by them, his mind in knots, his body quickly following."

Being a goalie is not the same thing as running a business and having to fire a team member whose vision does not align with its principles. But, running a business like Dreamshine and making sure every participant is treated with respect, dignity and a high moral standard takes focus and courage and the ability to mentally engage in a way that is similar to the athlete preparing mentally for a big game. A team member may be the best player out there scoring 60 points every game. But if his or her principles do not align with the organization's principles, there will eventually be a breakdown. If this star player treats the other team members in an unfair or disrespectful way, it no longer matters that he or she is scoring all the points. That kind of behavior does not fly. It works against the team's efforts and fails to unify the team. The team member I fired was doing the same thing. But in order to deflect problems and unify my dream team, I had to let him go.

One important lesson I learned through all of this is that when you focus on principles and leave feelings out of the picture, problems can be resolved more efficiently. In other words, it's okay to disagree and argue, as long as you disagree and argue with respect. That's how we can work through problems. Our principles keep us on the straight and narrow.

With principles and morals, nothing is impossible. But if we allow feelings to muddy the water, difficult situations do not improve. Nothing improves.

Take a look at this illustration. Analyze it for a few moments and then write what your initial impressions are and how they relate to where you are in your life right now.

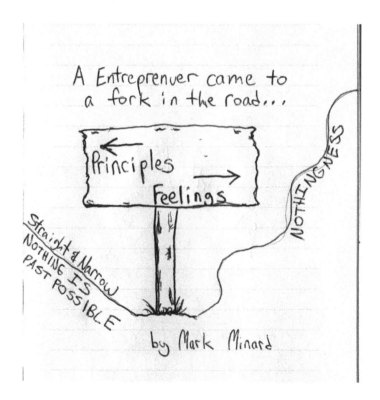

What do you think? How does the illustration help you understand the role feelings and principles play in growing a successful business, or relationship? Spend a few minutes recording some of the things that resonated with you as you read through this chapter.

_____

_____

_____

_____

_____

FAITH VS. FEELINGS

"No matter how big you grow, without a
strong foundation, it'll come crashing down."
—Dayne Gingrich

It wasn't raining when Noah built the ark.

In Genesis 6:13 God said to Noah, "I have determined to make an end of all flesh, for the earth is filled with violence through them. Behold, I will destroy them with the earth." God then goes on to tell Noah to make an ark out of gopher wood. He instructs him to make rooms and to cover the entire boat with pitch. God even gave Noah the exact dimensions of how big he wanted the ark to be. After mapping out the plans for the enormous boat, God then tells Noah that he will bring a devastating flood of waters upon the earth that will destroy every single living thing on it.

The flood would destroy everything and everyone, except for Noah and his family. Oh, and God mentioned that Noah would need to go out and collect two of every species of animal, bird, fish, etc. to save, too. And while on the ark during the duration of the flood, it was Noah's responsibility to keep them all alive.

Can you imagine how Noah was feeling at that moment? Not only had God himself personally contacted and spoke to Noah, but God told him that he would need to build a huge ark in order to save his family and two of every animal in existence. It seems like a lot to ask, doesn't it? But God knew that Noah was a follower. In fact, in Genesis 6:9, the Bible says: "Noah was a righteous man, blameless in his generation. Noah walked with God." As a result, Noah found favor in God's eyes (Genesis 6:8). So in other words, Noah lived by God's laws and followed his principles and God saw that. He then chose Noah to help him reboot Earth. But let's go back to how Noah must have felt. The Bible never says how he was feeling after being told to do such an enormous and what probably was deemed as crazy by everyone around him. But Noah did it anyway. Noah believed in God's principles and didn't care what other people thought. His faith and strength of character and morals got him through.

Noah's faith saved him.

Your faith is not a depiction of how you currently feel.

Now I am sure that at times, Noah felt silly, scared, challenged, and probably like he was making a big mistake. But his faith and how he was feeling are two completely different things. If there is one message you take away from reading this book, this might just be the most important one: Your faith is not a depiction of how you currently feel.

If you study some of the most articulate leaders in Christianity you will discover that they are all very much like Noah. And like the rest of us. In reading their works, you will find evidence that all of these great leaders and scholars experienced the same range of emotions and feelings that we do. C.S. Lewis (1898-1963), author, lecturer, and Christian, spoke about how there were times when he felt close to God and times when he felt almost numb or melancholy. But Lewis came to know God and recognized that it is normal for feelings to change.

C.S. Lewis wrote, "Though our feelings come and go, God's love for us does not."[26]

It is imperative to understand that faith in God is based on knowing, not feeling. I have come to learn that my faith is not a depiction of how I currently feel. In the course of a day, I can – and sometimes do – go through a wide range of feelings and emotions. But my faith never changes. Like C.S. Lewis, I go through different feelings, times of doubt, happiness, and divine epiphanies, but one thing remains constant. I know that Christ is with me regardless of how I feel. My peace comes from knowing this.

I used to think that I had to feel a certain way and if I didn't, I was doing something wrong or not doing something I should be. I used to think that if Christ was really in my heart, I would never have these feelings of doubt. But as I studied the Bible and the writings of Christian leaders and scholars, I realized that every disciple and major person in the Bible went through the same feelings. These people in the Bible even got to see Jesus working miracles and they still felt that way. I think God showed us these people with their doubts and feelings so that we would know that they were just like us – human.

> *Passion does not mean you are filled with feelings of constant joy every single second of every day. Passion is connected to your why.*

Faith is both a complicated and simple thing. Like Noah, I have had to learn to trust, believe and know that even though my feelings change, God does not. As a result, I have learned to pay closer attention to the gut feeling or instinct I sometimes get. This gut pull is a tension or feeling of unease I may experience repeatedly when I do not take action when I should. For example, this gut feeling tugged at me many times when I was not taking action to write this book. Even throughout the process of putting words on paper, I haven't "felt" it. Passion does not mean you are filled with feelings of constant joy every single second of every day. Passion is connected to your why. Once I realized this, I recognized that the foundation for my passion and principles is Christ. With that realization, came the ability to go way out of my comfort zone and write this book. I want to help you be a doer of your dreams, too. I want you to be the best you that you can be.

Think of a giant orchestra. Each musician is uniquely made to play a different instrument. They are trained to play, listen to each other, and work together to create a beautiful symphony. Each one of us is wonderfully made by God and uniquely different. Our job is to play as beautifully as we have been created to play, too. Our job is to go out into the world and listen to each other. Our job is to work together despite our failures, struggles, mistakes, new beginnings, heartaches, and friendships. It is our job to be the best we can we be.

It is your job to be the best you can be.

Being the best you can be is not based on feelings. It is based on a courage that comes from taking action day in and day out. It is based on doing the best you can regardless of how you feel. It all goes back to the very beginning of this book and when I said that knowledge and wisdom needs to be applied. Once applied, all of that knowledge and wisdom becomes power. From there, that power can be used in different ways. For me, having the power meant having more ability to serve other people. And that's why I wrote this book.

It wasn't raining when Noah built the ark.

CHARACTER IS EVERYTHING

A long your journey of 1,000 miles on your way to your vision manifested, your character will be challenged, questioned, and put to the test. In fact, I believe your success depends on it. Getting through character challenges takes courage, but once you are on the other side, you will discover that the pain and struggles were well worth it. One of the most valuable things I gained from my own adversity and experiences was the realization that I could help others who are faced with challenges. Along my way to success, I faced failures and adversity. I had some wins and losses. I discovered that character takes courage and leads to success. I learned that having success can lead to more courage. And I learned that you can't be truly successful without courage and a strong character.

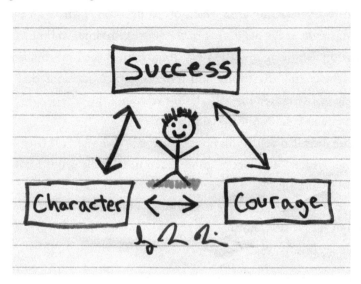

When I was doing research for this book, I did an Internet search for quotes about character. On this particular morning, there were more than 114 million websites where I could find what I was looking for. On one particular site, Brainyquote.com, there were 40 pages filled with quotes by famous people about character. I visited more websites and discovered that thousands of people had lots to say about character. In fact, I saw that there is no shortage of thoughts and advice about how to build character and what it means to have character. But when I asked myself what character looks like and how big of a role it plays when you are working toward your vision, I found it boils down to one thing: Courage. Eleanor Roosevelt once said, "People grow through experience if they meet life honestly and courageously. This is how character is built."

Character is built one decision at a time.

As I was growing Dreamshine, I learned that each and every decision I made affected the next set of decisions I would have to make. There was a direct correlation from decision to decision. I knew I needed to get things right at the beginning of the process in order to build a strong foundation. Knowing my WHY was important at the time, but knowing how to make ethically strong and morally sound decisions that would continue to strengthen my foundation was important, too.

Character is built one decision at a time.

Malcolm Gladwell, in his book *Blink: The Power of Thinking Without Thinking,* writes, "The key to good decision making is not knowledge. It is understanding. We are swimming in the former. We are desperately lacking in the latter." [27] I have found this to be true. As I was faced with seemingly impossible hurdles as I grew Dreamshine, I learned many valuable lessons.

> *"Life is a series of experiences, each one of which makes us bigger, even though sometimes it is hard to realize this. For the world was built to develop character, and we must learn that the setbacks and grieves which we endure helps us in our marching onward."*
> **—Henry Ford**

In addition to lessons about the bureaucratic rules and regulations, permits, laws, and ever-changing guidelines, I learned about human nature and the power of understanding. All of the things I learned were invaluable – and I am still using the lessons today – but the ones that made me search deep within myself until I found what I needed to move on were, by far, the most valuable. The tools I gained as I failed, feared, dwelled, and was paralyzed has help me get to where I am today. Ask any successful person you know how they grew as they got to where they are, and many will agree. It's what you learn along the way, but a big part of what you learn is about yourself. When character is called in to play, so much happens. Those who came before us have wisdom to share, and we should be taking advantage of their experiences. Henry Ford said, "Life is a series of experiences, each one of which makes us bigger, even though sometimes it is hard to realize this. For the world was built to develop character, and we must learn that the setbacks and grieves which we endure helps us in our marching onward."

There are many successful people who failed at first. The difference between failure and success, though, was that they did not give up. Each time someone told them they couldn't do something, wasn't smart enough or good enough, they carried on. Each time they fell, they picked themselves up and carried on. The fails and fears built character. And the decisions they made to learn and grow from the fails and fears built character.

When Thomas Edison was a young boy, his teachers told him he wasn't smart enough to learn anything. Oprah Winfrey was harassed and fired from her first job in television as a news anchor. Before Walt Disney became successful, he worked as a newspaper editor. He was fired for having a lack of imagination. When Steven Spielberg applied to the University of Southern California, School of Cinematic Arts, he was rejected multiple times. J.K Rowling was raising her child as a single mom on welfare when she started writing a book. Well...

- Thomas Edison did learn. In fact, he went on to invent the phonograph, electrical lamp, and movie camera, among other things – all inventions that changed our world. At the time of his death, he held more than 1,000 patents.
- Oprah Winfrey did not let harassment and being fired stop her. She learned to be resilient and is known as the queen of television talk shows. Her media empire is worth close to $3 billion.

- If Walt Disney became discouraged by what his employers said about him, most of our childhood memories would not be the same. The animator and entrepreneur went on to become a successful innovator in animation and theme park design. He and his brother, Roy, co-founded The Walt Disney Company, or Disney, which is the second largest broadcasting and cable company in the world.

- Steven Spielberg did not give up and went on to make many blockbuster movies, including "Jaws," "Back to the Future," "Schindler's List," "Men in Black," "Saving Private Ryan," and "Shrek." Enough said.

- Have you read the Harry Potter books? Have you see the Harry Potter movies or visited the theme park? If yes, then you have J.K. Rowling to thank.[28] Thank goodness her character was stronger than her fears and failures.

Do you see why I keep saying that character is important? These are just a few examples. All you have to do is search online and you will find hundreds more examples of people – in all walks of life – who used adversity and challenging situations to grow their character. I have discovered that character counts in business. But, I have also learned that it counts when it comes to my marriage, my family, my health, my finances, my relationships, and my personal growth. The foundation that every area of my life is built upon is character.

Character is that important.

COURAGE

"Many a man's reputation would not know
his character if they met on the street."
—**Elbert Hubbard**, American writer

The foundation that every area of my life is built upon is character. Through everything I have done, and am still doing, I rely on God for strength. We all have our own impossible situations and things that God has put in our lives to overcome, but that's just His glory in action. Working through the challenges has taught me to walk with God. Miracles don't occur within the comfort zone. It takes being broken to have a breakthrough. In the last chapter, we talked about character. I said that character takes courage and courage leads to success. Experiencing success leads to having more courage. You can't be truly successful without courage and a strong character.

Amen.

> Miracles don't occur within the comfort zone.
> It takes being broken to have a breakthrough.

God helps us out in this department. In the Bible, he encourages us to be strong and courageous. In fact, in the book of Joshua, He repeats the phrase, "be strong and courageous" a few times. We know that when God repeats something, He wants us to take notice.

Joshua studied under Moses for many years and, after Moses died, God sent Joshua to lead the Israelites across the Jordan River to the Promised Land. Which he does. But God never stopped encouraging him. In Joshua 1:6, God says, "Be strong and courageous, for you shall cause this people to inherit the land that I swore to their fathers to give them." In verse 7, God says, "Only be strong and very courageous, being careful to do according to all the law that Moses my servant commanded you. Do not turn from it to the right hand or to the left, that you may have good success wherever you go." So God is telling Joshua to make good decisions and to follow the law and do the right things. God is encouraging Joshua to be strong and brave. Then in verse 9, God says it again: "Have I not commanded you? Be strong and courageous. Do not be frightened, and do not be dismayed, for the LORD your God is with you wherever you go."

Great advice then.

Great advice now.

So how does God's advice to Joshua translate into advice for us today? Like I said earlier, miracles don't occur within our comfort zone. Do you think Joshua was comfortable leading the Israelites across the Jordan River? There were many obstacles before him, but he trusted God and carried on. The obstacles I faced made me fearful. At times I doubted my abilities and became paralyzed with anxiety. But I kept my focus on my WHY. I set my sights on setting up a place for people with disabilities and the vision of helping people who deserve a good life was my guiding light. I learned that no matter how hard things may seem at the time, I have it in me to be courageous. I learned to lean on God.

I learned to be brave.

Now it's time for you to go back to your vision, to your WHY. Write a few lines about what it is you want to do.

_____

_____

_____

_____

_____

Now think about your obstacles. What are the things that are getting in your way? Narrow them down to your top three. List them here:

_____

_____

_____

_____

_____

Good. Now use the graphic organizer on the next page to map out how you can help yourself get to where you want to be. How will you overcome your obstacles?

Success	Character	Courage

CHARACTER VS. REPUTATION

"Character is like a tree and reputation like a shadow. The shadow is what we think of it; the tree is the real thing."
—Abraham Lincoln

Let's talk about overnight success.

Many of us, including me, have been caught up in wanting to achieve success right now. The thought of becoming an overnight sensation is intoxicating. But, in reality – and with the exception of winning the lottery (which has its own set of issues) – there is no such thing as an overnight success. I will elaborate more about success in the next chapter. For now, let's talk about reputation.

The average success story takes, well, as long as it takes. I think it varies from one successful person to the next. However, I do think there are things that can help move the process along, and I have already covered two of them: Character and courage. I also think there is one big thing that can sabotage success. That one big thing is reputation.

These days everyone talks about how important branding is. And while that can be true, character is much more important. Character is the foundation that your brand is built upon. Without a strong character, a brand is nothing more than a shiny wrapping on a sub-par product – kind of the hare in the children's story, "The Tortoise and the Hare." I like to use this fable to exemplify the difference between character and reputation.

In this illustration, the tortoise represents character and the hare is reputation. In the fable, originally written by Aesop, the hare is flashy and fast and way more talented than the tortoise. That's how everyone sees him. That's mainly because that's how he sees himself. He also goes around bragging about how great he is. The tortoise, on the other hand, is not as attractive, not as popular, and no one really pays all that much attention to him. In the story, the hare is confident and rude. He has a reputation for being fast and cocky. His brand, if you will, screams, "Look at me. I'm a winner. I am better than you." One day, the tortoise gets tired of the hare's bragging and challenges him to a race. Of course, all the animals in the forest gather around to watch.

"On your mark. Get set. Go!"

The race began and the hare runs down the road. He was way ahead and began taunting the tortoise.

"Slow poke," he called. "How do you expect to win if you can go any faster than that."

Now, the hare is all about reputation. He is lazy and arrogant and lacks character. He saw a shady spot on the side of the road and decided to take a rest. He figured he had plenty of time for a nap. It would take the tortoise forever to get to where he was resting. But, the tortoise kept walking at his slow and steady pace. He didn't stop to rest. He was determined and resilient and willing to go against the odds. The tortoise had the faith to believe that could win the race. So, he focused on his vision manifested, or the finish line. He knows that even if the hare beat him there, as long as he kept moving and his eye on the prize, he knew he was a winner.

Winners have character.

The tortoise kept going until he got to the finish line and crossed it. The animals cheered so loudly for the tortoise that they woke the hare up. The hare jumped up and began running toward the finish line, but it was already too late. The tortoise had won.

The hare misjudged the tortoise. Believing he would win, but not putting in the work, caused him to lose the race. This is a children's fable and it teaches a few lessons.

Don't brag.

Slow and steady wins the race.

If I could add more to the fable, it would be this. The hare lost the race and just walks away. He does not commit to trying harder, to growing, developing, or being accountable for his behavior before and during the race. He does not apologize to the tortoise or the animals in the forest. Instead, he becomes a sore loser and accuses the tortoise of cheating.

Helen Keller said, "Character cannot be developed in ease and quiet. Only through experience of trial and suffering can the soul be strengthened, ambition inspired, and success achieved."

> *Character did not just win the race, it is a champion and wins the marathon of life. Character knows that being a champion is a lifelong journey.*

In my version of the story, the tortoise wins the race and does not waste energy gloating or bragging about it. He knows he won because he kept his eyes on his vision and did not stray. He was brave and took action and won.

It is much easier to act like the hare, isn't it? Bragging when you're at the top of your game and getting angry when things don't go your way takes no self-control at all. And even though the tortoise's inner voice may have said to him, "Hey, buddy, that hare is walking all over you," his character knew better. Character did not just win the race, it is a champion and wins the marathon of life. Character knows that being a champion is a lifelong journey.

Character looks a lot like courage, which looks a lot like applying knowledge for all that is good.

My good friend Chance Miller is the chief editor of my podcast, "Elevating Beyond." I have had the honor of mentoring him recently and would like to share something that happened to him that put his character to the test.

It was about 7:30 a.m. on a Thursday in April. I was juggling getting my kids ready for school, responding to a situation at Dreamshine, and help my wife with our three-month-old baby son, Gilbert. As I rushed around, I noticed that I had several missed calls and text messages on my phone. They were all from Chance. Knowing that he usually does not call or text repeatedly raised a red flag and I quickly, in between everything I was doing, texted to let him know that we would be able to talk in about 30 minutes.

When Chance and I talked, he told me that his supervisor was angry because he had decided not to renew his contract with the military. Chance had created a new app called "Revation" and wanted more time to work on it. Chance said that he just couldn't force himself to like something. What he was working on wasn't his WHY and he needed to move on. Chance told me that his supervisor thought he was insane for leaving a stable job for something he called imaginary. I worked with Chance on his app, and it was his vision manifested.

Chance's supervisors attacked at every angle. They told him that he made it this far in the military and should continue with it, while working on "Revation" on the side. They watched him closely, sure that his performance would suffer as the date for his last day approached. They told him that his dream didn't work and that he was going to come crawling back to the Navy, but the Navy was not going to accept him back in.

Does this sound like something you've heard before? Walt Disney? Thomas Edison? Steven Spielberg? Oprah Winfrey? While the negative people and comments may not be the same, the message is that what Chance was doing didn't matter. But I knew that it did, and so did he. Chance even told me that his supervisors tried to make an example of him by throwing more and more tasks his way. Then, as he was grinding on two different things, he was asked to put on his dress uniform and conduct a meeting that had missed the week before. Chance proudly shared with me that he did such a great job running the meeting that everyone requested that he conduct them from then on. His supervisors tried to humiliate him, but it had backfired. Chance felt angry and sad at the games they were playing with him, but he continued to work hard and do the best he could.

After he had shared his story about what was happening at work with me, I told him not to sacrifice his character for mediocrity. To help him understand exactly what I meant, I shared something with him that had happened to me at Dreamshine.

Remember the team member I had to fire because of his poor attitude and unwillingness to be grow and be in line with our principles? Well, unfortunately, this person communicated with another team member on social media about what had happened. Both people had been let go because they were unwilling to grow and be a part of the Dreamshine team. As they began sharing their experiences, they started posting lies about my character and business. After each of their terminations, I had paid additional medical premiums and other incentives that I was not obligated to do. This made what they were doing online even more hurtful. I found out about what was going on through other employees who were connected with them.

Here's what I faced.

There were lies and slanderous comments about my character and Dreamshine floating around on the Internet. This made me angry. This made me want to retaliate and post a series of replies to prove the comments untrue. I wanted to tell my side of the story. Instead, I thanked my team members for calling my attention to what was happening and then made the conscious decision to wait 24 hours before deciding what to do.

The 24-hour rule is imperative at times when I know my feelings are overloaded.

At the time, I knew I was not able to make a good choice about what I would do. I was way too emotional. I was angry. I was hurt. I felt like I had been slapped in the face. These are the moments, according to Martin Luther King, Jr., when true character is put to the test. He said it this way: "The ultimate test of a man is not where he stands in moments of comfort and moments of convenience, but where he stands in moments of challenge and moments of controversy."

The 24-hour rule is imperative at times when I know my feelings are overloaded.

After 24 hours had gone by, I jogged. I prayed. I focused on my WHY and thought about all of the Dreamshine families and individuals with special needs. I thought about how we were growing and providing amazing opportunities through the years. I thought about how we continued to blossom to new levels each year. I met with my head administrator the next day and talked about what was going on and what I was thinking. I wanted to make sure we were all on the same page. We talked and made sure everyone knew what was happening. They all knew the truth, but I wanted to make sure everything was on the table. Then, do you know what I posted on social media in response?

Nothing.

Was this easy for me to do?

No.

Was it the right thing to do?

Yes.

At our next team meeting, I spoke about what had happened and explained the facts of the events and what was posted online by the two former team members. I did not say horrible things about the people who posted the lies. I did say that the events were unfortunate and showed a poor display of character. I said that we would move on and continue changing people's lives at Dreamshine. My reputation was at stake, but my character won out. I gave it to God. I knew deep down that God would reveal the strong foundation of my character vs. the false reputation that had been portrayed online.

Years ago if this same thing had happened, I can honestly say that I would not have reacted in the same way. I might have given into my feelings and emotions. In an effort to protect my reputation, I probably would have retaliated on the social media site, which in turn would have most likely created more and more drama. I have learned to depend on my WHY and have built a strong character with courage. Instead of feeding the negativity, I starved it.

This event has taught me many things about myself. What has it taught you? Have you had a similar experience? How did you handle it? How did you wish you handled it?

_____

_____

_____

_____

A strong character is like an iceberg. You see a small piece of it above the water. The bulk of the iceberg is below the surface. And when reputation meets character, character always wins. We all know what happened to the Titanic.

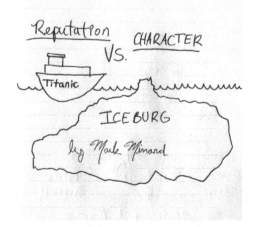

SUCCESS

"Fruits speak louder than words."
—Mark Minard

Thomas Edison was a great inventor. But it was not uncommon for him to be ridiculed by the media and critics for failing over a thousand times during the process of inventing the light bulb. One day, at a media event, a reporter asked him what he thought about his critics. Edison did not say a word. He simply walked over and flipped on the light bulb.

Fruits speak louder than words.

Joshua obeyed God and trusted that when he needed help, it would be there. When Joshua and the Israelites got to the banks of the Jordan River, God dried up the waters and they walked across.

Fruits speak louder than words.

Lies and slanderous comments on a social media site that were personally hurtful to both Dreamshine and me were met with nothing. No retaliation. No comments. No attention.

Fruits speak louder than words.

I do realize that the saying is actually "actions speak louder than words." That expression is appropriate for all three of the above situations, as well. However, when your hard work, courage, strong character, principles, and WHY are realized, success is your reward. It is the fruit that people see.

In success, as in life, walking is more important than talking. When you walk the talk, you are showing the world who you really are. You are displaying your strength of character and not showing off your unreliable and weak reputation. A strong character, with the right amount of courage, leads to success.

Dreamshine is my fruit.

When we first met Solid at the beginning of this book, we learned that he knows all about bravery and hard work. He knows the importance of following through and trusting that your WHY is bigger than your doubts and fears. In my research for writing this book, I learned so much about so many people and how integrity and a strong character leads to significant success.

I want to tell you about a few of them.

SIGNIFICANT SUCCESS: PART ONE

"Be relentless about your integrity and you will discover success."
—Mark Minard

H aving significant success is not about having money, fame, or power. Significant success is more than money, more than fame, more than power. The word *significant* is a Latin word meaning important or notable. It means consequential, or having consequences. So when I pair the word *significant* with the word *success,* I am talking about being successful in a way that changes or helps others. Being significantly successful means using your success to affect other people in a positive way. Bono, the lead singer of U2 is a great example of how someone can use their wealth and influence to change the world.

Born Paul David Hewson, Bono's countless devoted fans from throughout the world love him for much more than his music. This man is a humanitarian and champion for the world's poor. He worked in a feeding camp with his wife, Alison Stewart, and the charity, World Vision, in Ethopia. After that, during the 1990s, he campaigned with Greenpeace. Ten years later, he gathered other artists and actors to campaign toward ending Third World debt. Bono works tirelessly to build awareness and try to end AIDS and poverty in Africa and in doing so has co-founded two lobbying organizations: DATA (Debt, Aid, Trade, Africa) in 2002, and the ONE Campaign to Make Poverty History in 2004. Throughout the 2000s, he and Rogan Gregory, a fashion designer, created a clothing line for men and women to promote fair trade and sustainable growth. The clothes they design and make are manufactured by residents of poor communities in facilities that are environmentally friendly and nothing like the sweatshops we hear so much about. And these are just a handful of the things he has done over the years. His energy and commitment is contagious and Bono has teamed up with many notable singers, songwriters, actors, and statesmen to champion causes for the good of humankind.

Bono is wealthy in possessions and worth a lot of money. In 2012, ABC News stated that Bono was about to surpass the net worth of Paul McCartney, who at the time was the wealthiest rock star in the world. Bono was reportedly worth more than $1.5 billion at the time. Sure he makes good investments and U2 has sold millions of albums, but Bono is also one of those celebrities who use their wealth and power and intelligence for good. He is a great example of what I mean by significant success. He is using fame and fortune in a good way. Bono is following what God has put in his heart. He knows God's plan is a lifelong journey. That's what I mean by significant success. It is using the individual plan God has for each one of us. The plan he puts into our hearts. It is taking that plan and spending your life working toward that goal.[29]

Bono does so much good in the world. But you don't have to be rich and famous to follow God's plan for your life. You just have to be a good listener and follow God's instructions. When God put Dreamshine on my heart, I listened. It has become my life's journey. Dreamshine is my life's work. I may not be wealthy in possessions, but my family and my work at Dreamshine has made me a rich man in many other ways. Barnabas was like that, too. Mentioned first in Acts, he is another great example of someone who achieved significant success.

Barnabas is one of my favorite people in the Bible. He was not someone who was always in the spotlight, but he played a huge role in spreading the Gospel in the early days of the church. According to Acts 4:36, Barnabas' name means "son of encouragement." In the scriptures, Barnabas is seen as someone who provided help, encouragement, comfort and wisdom to everyone around him. In fact, he was there after Saul encountered Jesus in the desert and became Paul. That's amazing because Paul…when he was Saul…was a bad guy. Before he became one of Jesus' apostles, Paul was known as Saul of Tarsus, and he was one of Christianity's biggest and most outspoken enemies. He was merciless and persecuted the church every chance he got. The amazing thing about God is that he can change anyone.

> *"When you encourage others, you in the process are encouraged because you're making a commitment and difference in that person's life. Encouragement really does make a difference."*
> **—Zig Ziglar**

When Saul saw the resurrected Jesus on Damascus Road, he converted and then became one of the church's biggest advocates. But because of his zealous condemnation of God as Saul, the apostles were hesitant to meet with him and welcome him into their lives. But Luke writes in Acts 9:27, "But Barnabas took him and brought him to the apostles. He told them how Saul on his journey had seen the Lord and that the Lord had spoken to him, and how in Damascus he had preached fearlessly in the name of Jesus."

Barnabas went to bat for Paul and got the apostles to see that he was a different person. God had changed Saul's heart when he converted and became Paul. And it was Barnabas who encouraged the apostles to accept him. Barnabas was key in unifying the apostles and the rest, as you know, is history.

It is through the encouragement of others that we can become rich. Noted author and motivational speaker, Zig Ziglar once said, "When you encourage others, you in the process are encouraged because you're making a difference in that person's life. Encouragement really does make a difference."

That's my point. Being a significant success means getting rich by encouraging others, by giving hope to others, and by taking action. To do that, we need to listen to and follow the individual plan God places in each one of our hearts. We also need to transform that plan into a way of life and make it our life long journey.

To help you remember this, fill in the graphic organizer below.

In the first chapter of this book, I touched briefly upon how reading pulled me up and out of a life of partying, drugs, alcohol, broken bones, and jail. In short, I had passed out and found myself in jail with a broken jaw and fractured eye socket. I had been charged with a DUI, or Driving Under the Influence. At that time in my earlier life, I was involved with drugs and many other bad things. It turns out, my childhood friend whom I will call John, had a similar experience. John wound up in jail with a DUI about a month after me. We were on probation and did community service together. Our probation and community service work, however, did not stop us from partying, drugs and alcohol – among other things. Through all of that, though, our strong faith that had been built when we were teenagers remained and we always talked about God. After a time, we began to change our lives. We talked more and more about God and grew closer to Him over the years. John ended up going to college where he studied and became an elementary school teacher. Here's where the story gets even better.

John has since achieved significant success.

As teenagers, I remember John being so great at doing impressions, like Shaggy, the goateed, cowardly slacker in the Scooby-Doo animated television series. John did many other impressions, too. And he is still doing them. But instead of using his talents to entertain, he is using them to teach. John brings his imagination into his classroom. He even buys costumes and props to teach lessons about Albert Einstein and Abraham Lincoln, to name a few. In doing this, John makes history come alive and makes learning more interesting and fun for his students. He brings the lessons he teaches to life by going above and beyond. As a result, the kids love him and they look forward to learning. They also remember what he teaches because he is getting them to use their imaginations, as well. His costumes and wild impressions go a long way in helping kids comprehend and remember. This is what makes him a significant success.

The point is, you do not have to be an entrepreneur or a celebrity or an author to be significantly successful. You just need to:

1. follow what you are continually being called by God to be and do;
2. have the faith to be awesome at it, even when it means you might make a fool of yourself and even if it means you fail (and I've said it before and will say it again: you are never a failure if you try); and
3. never, ever, ever give up.

Always ask yourself, "What would Solid do?"

SIGNIFICANT SUCCESS: PART TWO

"Number one: Put God first. Put God first in everything you do."
—Denzel Washington

O n Sunday, May 10, 2015, Denzel Washington gave an inspirational commencement speech to the graduating class at Dillard University in New Orleans, Louisiana. He told the crowd of students, their families and friends to put God first. He told them to fail big. He told them to aspire to do more than make a living. He told them to aspire to make a difference.

Denzel Washington was born in Mount Vernon, New York in 1954. His mother was a beautician and his father was a Pentecostal minister. From 1982 to 1988, he played Dr. Philip Chandler in NBC's hit medical television series *St. Elsewhere*. Denzel Washington has starred in many major films, including *Malcolm X, Glory, The Taking of Pelham 1 2 3,*

Philadelphia, The Book of Eli, and *Safe House.* He lives in Los Angeles, California with his wife, Pauletta Washington, and their four children.[30] Denzel started his speech by saying that he was going to keep it short. I watched that speech on YouTube and am here to tell you that it is so inspirational. I love what he says about significant success and pursuing your dreams.

According to Denzel Washington:

1. Put God first in everything.
2. Fail big. Dream big. In other words, take chances and don't be afraid to fail. Don't be afraid to go outside the box.
3. In order to achieve your goals, apply discipline and consistency.
4. Hard work works.
5. Busyness does not always equal effectiveness. Just because you're doing a lot more doesn't mean you're getting a lot done.
6. It's not how much you have, it's what you do with what you have. That's real success. That's significant success!
7. Real success comes from helping others. Denzel said that on your way up to the top, as you succeed, turn around and pull the person behind you up.

> *"Everything I've accomplished, everything you think I have – and I have a few things - everything that I have is by the grace of God. Understand that. It's a gift."*
> **—Denzel Washington**

8. When you go to bed at night, put your slippers way underneath your bed. That way, in the morning when you wake up, you have to get on your knees to reach them. And while you're down there, he said, say thank you to God. Thank you for grace, thank

you for mercy, thank you for understanding, wisdom, kindness, peace, prosperity, and parents.

9. And toward the end of his speech, Denzel said, "You'll never see a U-Haul behind a hearse." That's because it's not how much you have, it's what you do with what you have. Don't just aspire to make a living. Aspire to make a difference.

At one point during his short speech, Denzel said, "Everything I've accomplished, everything you think I have – and I have a few things. Everything that I have is by the grace of God. Understand that. It's a gift."

Can you see why I love this man's speech? It truly speaks to everything I believe in. So when I watched it, I knew I had to share it with you. The bottom line is: We were all put on this Earth for a reason, and that is to be the best YOU. Being the best you means living your life to achieve significant success. Being your best means not being afraid to be terrible.

Remember when I said that at the beginning of this book? I explained how not being afraid to be terrible released me from fear. I have learned to allow my passion to lead me and as a result, my fear no longer leads me. I have learned to allow my WHY to lead me. I have learned to listen to and be led by God. But that doesn't mean I'm never afraid. In your journey for significant success, you will feel fear. You will face adversity. But you cannot let it stop you from being the best you. The purpose for sharing my story with you is to show you that I am not special. I am just like you.

You are just like me.

I face fear on a daily basis. I choose not to let it stop me. You can do the same. That means saying yes to scary. Even if fear has stopped you, or still stops you, the most important thing is to never give up. Remember: We are all capable of being special.

In Spring of 2015, Michael McGreevy was a guest on one of our *Elevating Beyond* podcasts. On the show, he described what he was like in high school and how fear got the better of him and strangled every hope he had for being athletic, artistic, social, and successful. He said he was very anxious and would do anything to avoid having a panic attack. He begged his parents to let him stay home from high school because he was terrified. Michael's anxiety caused him to suffer and to lose out on so much. When he miraculously graduated from high school and went on to college, he used many avoidance-type coping behaviors, like alcohol, to get through. Those behaviors turned out to be more hurtful than helpful. After graduating from college, Michael felt like a failure. He was living at his parents' house and they told him had to get a job. Which he did. He and a friend began working as laborers on a construction project. One day they were on the second floor of one of the houses they were building when Michael's friend accidentally stepped backward off the edge of the floor and fell two stories. Michael was right there when it happened. He got his boss' phone, and immediately called 911. Despite his anxiety, Michael went down to the basement, where his friend had fallen. Working to keep the young man alive, Michael performed CPR until the paramedics arrived to take him to the hospital. Later that evening, Michael and his boss went to the hospital. His friend's family was waiting outside the room where his friend had just been pronounced dead. Michael describes being there and witnessing how distraught his friend's mother was. How she literally fell apart and kept asking what happened to her son.

"And to this day, that was the worst day of my life," recalls Michael.

Shortly after the accident, Michael became depressed. So when his family decided to take a trip to the ocean, he thought it might be good for him to get away. While swimming, Michael got caught up in the undertow. He fought the undertow for 30 terrifying and exhausting minutes before he could make his way back to the beach. Physically and emotionally weary, Michael looked out over the water and saw two young girls - family friends - caught way out in the undertow. Too physically exhausted to help, Michael struggled in his mind with what to do. Deciding that he never wanted to see a parent suffer the way he saw his friend's mother suffer when he died, Michael pushed himself and swam out to meet the two young girls. Clinging to each other, the three eventually made it back to shore. Michael used the tragedy of his friend's death to save those two young girls from drowning. For the first time in his life he felt he had something to give the world.

"I do believe that it was God who whispered that message to me," said Michael. "See, this is who I made you to be and not what you believed before about yourself."

Armed with a more confident self-image, Michael began studying leadership and started his own coaching business to help others overcome fear and learn to believe in themselves. And while starting his business did not occur overnight, Michael now devotes his life to supporting others and living a life of meaning.

> *It's an adventure to follow Christ day in and day out, and do things that scare you.*

(For information about Michael, go to http://mcgreevyleadership.com.) And since the podcast aired, Michael and I have made a connection and have continued to encourage each other. In fact, one morning not too long ago, he sent me a text: "Do something that scares you today." I wrote that sentence on a post-it note and taped it to the steering wheel of my car. He somehow knew the exact thing I needed to hear at the exact moment I needed to hear it.

When Michael sent me the text message encouraging me to do something that scared me that day, I already had something in mind. After months of very little sleep, my wife and I had an argument that got out of hand. Stress of a new baby coupled with a severe lack of sleep fueled a small disagreement into a full, blown-out war. I can't even remember what we disagreed about. All I could remember was how hurtful some of the things I said to my wife were. So when I received Michael's text, I knew that I had to apologize to her.

It's an adventure to follow Christ day in and day out and do things that scare you.

Isn't it?

The first thing I did was text Michael. I wrote that my wife and I had had an argument and that I needed to apologize to her. I did this so that he would hold me accountable. Then I texted my wife. I told her I loved her and that I was sorry. My wife called me and I apologized again. She told me she was sorry and that she loves me. We eventually found ourselves laughing about it. It was awesome. What began as scary for me, ended up being fine. I said yes to scary and things worked out.

So I dare you to write these words on an index card or post-it note, or create a screen saver for your computer. The important thing is to place this sentence where you will see it during the day:

DO SOMETHING THAT SCARES YOU TODAY.

Be intentional. Think about this sentence. Live one day like this. Then another. Then another. Then try to live the rest of your life like this. This is what I believe faith in action truly is. Following Christ every day is an adventure. It involves doing things that are scary. It means never giving up. It's never too late to start NOT giving up. Even if that thing has not manifested itself yet, I would rather die hoping rather than giving up. This, to me, is a life lived in faith.

You will feel fear.

You will face adversity.

Do not let it stop you from being the best you.

FAITH IN ACTION

"For the Spirit God gave us does not make us timid,
but gives us power, love, and self-discipline."
—2 Timothy 1:7

God has created us to be fearless. This I know. He wants us to stand up and fight for the strengths he has given each one of us. He wants us to control our thoughts and stand strong against the enemy. I recite 2 Timothy 1:7 when I need to fight my fears and anxieties. Find a Bible verse that speaks to you. Memorize it. Write it on cards and tape them where you can see them. Recite it. Share it. Remember that God does not want us to be afraid. He has made us fearless.

One of my favorite movies of all time is *The Goonies*. In this 1985 adventure film, a group of misfit teens band together to save their homes from a group of investors who want to bulldoze them and turn the land into a golf course. They do this by finding an old pirate's map and then setting out to find One-Eyed Willie's ancient treasure. This group of kids got together, made a plan, and went after what they knew in their hearts would save their town.

> Impossible is where every great adventure begins.

They had a WHY.

They went after scary.

This group of young people remind me a lot of Jesus' disciples. They were a group of misfits with a WHY, too. Their adventure was a scary one. What the Goonies (which is what they called themselves) set out to do seemed impossible. What the disciples were doing seemed impossible at the time, as well. But I am here to say that impossible is where every great adventure begins. (And seriously, if you haven't seen *The Goonies*, stop reading and watch it now. Well finish reading the book, then go rent it.)

Another movie hero that brings to mind how being fearless, following your WHY, and going after scary is what we have to do is Indiana Jones. What a hero, right? We first meet Dr. Indiana Henry Jones, Jr. in the adventure film *The Raiders of the Lost Ark.* In the movie he is an archaeologist, a professor at a university, and an adventurer. When he discovers where the Cross of Coronado is, he goes on a quest to recover it from the people whom he suspected were grave robbers. Along the way, he is thrown in a pit of snakes, goes face-to-face with a lion, and finds himself in many sticky and unusually difficult and scary situations. I won't spoil the movie for you if you haven't seen it (but seriously, if you haven't, you need to). I will say that something interesting I discovered while writing this book is a small connection between Indiana Jones and Jesus.

When Jones came face-to-face with a lion, he was forced to use his bull whip. When Jesus came face-to-face with the money-changers and merchants in the temple, John 2:15 tells us that "he made a whip out of cords, and drove all from the temple courts, both sheep and cattle; he scattered the coins of the money changers and overturned their tables." Both Indiana Jones, the fictional movie character, and Jesus, the real-life hero, went after scary. They fearlessly went after scary because it was the right thing to do.

For people like you and I, doing things that scare us every day will help us discover what faith in action feels like. When you seek the knowledge and then apply that knowledge, you will be equipped to face the scary. Facing the scary will get you to faith in action. Faith in action will lead you on the greatest adventures of your life.

Trust me. I know.

This book started out with a pencil, a notepad, and a stick figure drawing of a dude named Solid with a dream to be the modern day Barnabas. It is my hope that, like Barnabas, I have encouraged you to break free from fear, find your WHY, and keep doing. And if you want to get a bull whip, why not? You were put on Earth for adventure. Equip yourself with the tools you need.

After all, isn't this what Solid would do?

WHAT WOULD SOLID DO?

→ ← → ←

*"So now it's time for you to landscape the knowledge
you have discovered from this book and plant seeds
of greatness into others by taking action."*
—**Mark Minard**

Reading changed my life. It helped me find my WHY and get
me right where I am today. In *Solid's Elevational Journey* I
talked about how Solid crosses his seemingly unsurmountable
mountain ranges of fear and failure. I showed you how he fuels his
adventure with knowledge and application. I discussed how he digs
in and climbs to the top, while dealing with whatever gets in his way.
Solid never settles. The whole time, I told you how Solid is focused
on his vision. He battles storms, setbacks, self-doubt, negativity, fear,
and anxiety. Solid remains fixed on reaching his goal. That's how he

gets to the top of his mountain of fears. That's how he becomes a significant success.

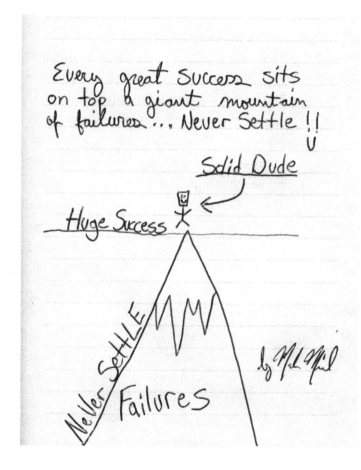

That's how I become a significant success and that's how you become a significant success, too.

The most important take-aways from this book cannot be put into a neat list. That's because we are all different and what strikes me as being important may or may not be what you think is important. That's okay. But I want to hit the highlights for you. I want you to close this book and have the knowledge to create your life's path. I want you to change your mindset and discover that the circumstances will follow. I want you to landscape the knowledge you have discovered from this book and plant seeds of greatness into others by taking action.

I want you to be a significant success.

Finding your WHY is big. One of Solid's biggest pieces of advice is to reach up in the sky and pull your dream down. Then you will find where your vision is found. I call that being intentional and willing. Both take guts but are necessary as you climb your mountains of fear and doubt. To identify your WHY, you must listen to God's inner voice, his individual plan for you. Think, meditate, envision. The dream must be grasped before it can be manifested. One of God's plans for my life was to create a caring and supportive environment for adults with special needs, the likes of which wasn't there before. That was my vision. It became my WHY only after I dreamed about it, talked about it, and envisioned it. Then I believed it was possible. Then it became possible.

Find your dream. Ponder and meditate on it. Ask God for guidance. Then be quiet and listen for as long as it takes. Make the intentional choice to walk away from and abandon the voices in your head that are telling you that you are not good enough. Banish those voices from your kingdom. They have no place in your life anymore. They have no place in your WHY.

Focus on what you want and where you want to be and take one intentional step at a time. Never give up. Win one war and move on to the next one. Once you start winning those battles, you will be changed forever.

Go you.

The best two-step business plan ever is to stop planning and start doing. Then keep doing. Take the theories and suggestions and stories and motivational stories out of the pages of this book and carry them with you into the real world.

That's what Solid would do.

*"If you wait for perfect conditions,
you will never get anything done."*
—Ecclesiastes 11:4 (TLB)

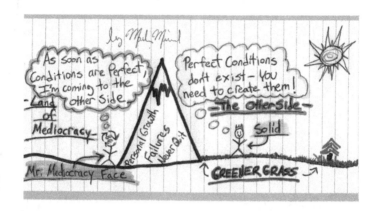

Pay attention. Count on your faith. Count on the fact that God is orchestrating everything about your life. Then move those mountains. Start now!

That's what Solid would do.

Solid rises above mediocrity. He uses his abilities and tools to step out of mediocre and into the life he wants. He melts his fears by standing his ground, keeping his eyes on his dream, and following his light. That light propels him forward and upward, but it also causes him to stop and reach back to pull others up with him.

Be a success, but be a significant success.

Remember to always be open and honest and human. Character growth is an ongoing thing and something that we all must be intentional about. With great fortitude, put your principles into action. Keep in mind that takes practice and courage. When something is difficult for me to do, I have to be completely intentional in order to do it. That means focusing on my principles, my values, and my why. That's what you need to do.

That's what Solid would do.

Reading changed my life. I hope reading this book has changed yours.

ENDNOTES

1   Panic Disorder and Agoraphobia, Symptoms. The Anxiety and
    Depression Association of America Retrieved on November 18,
    2014, from http://www.adaa.org/understanding-anxiety/panic-
    disorder-agoraphobia/symptoms

2   Living and Thriving, College Students, Fact. The Anxiety and
    Depression Association of America, retrieved on November 18,
    2014, from http://www.adaa.org/finding-help/helping-others/
    college-students/facts

3   Tartakovsky, M. (2008). Depression and Anxiety Among College
    Students. *Psych Central.* Retrieved on November 23, 2014, from
    http://psychcentral.com/lib/depression-and-anxiety-among-
    college-students/0001425

4   New International Bible

5   Retrieved on November 21, 2014 from http://aspe.hhs.gov/daltcp/
    reports/adultdayOH.pdf.

6   Retrieved on November 22, 2014 from http://dictionary.reference.
    com/browse/visionary.

7   Baroncini-Moe, Susan. "Change the Way You See Fear and
    Change Your Life," Lifehack.com. Retrieved on December 21,
    2014 from http://www.lifehack.org/articles/lifestyle/change-the-
    way-you-see-fear-and-change-your-life.html

8   "Linus' Security Blanket" Retrieved on December 21, 2014 from
    http://peanuts.wikia.com/wiki/Linus%27_security_blanket

9   Alan Alda. Retrieved on December 27, 2014 from http://www.
    dreambuilders.com.au/inspirations/about-awareness .

10 http://www.merriam-webster.com/dictionary/intention. Retrieved
    December 27, 2014.

11 Warren, Rick. *The Purpose Driven Life,* Zondervan, Grand Rapids,
    Michigan, 2002, page 10.

12 Hill, Napoleon. *Outwitting the Devil,* Sterling Publishing, 1938

13 "Spam," urban dictionary.com. Retrieved January 21,
    2015 from http://www.urbandictionary.com/define.
    php?term=SPAM&defid=2068223

14 Lessard, Tom, "5 Ways to stop spam email today." The Online
    Privacy Blog, July 31, 2013. Retrieved January 21, 2015 from
    https://www.abine.com/blog/2013/stop-spam-email-today/

15 Hinckley, David. "MTVs reality pioneer 'The Real World' starts
    its 30th season," *New York Daily News,* December 14, 2014.
    Retrieved January 30, 2015 from http://www.nydailynews.
    com/entertainment/tv/mtv-real-world-starts-30th-season-
    article-1.2041075

16 "Brain Tracy," Amazon.com. Retrieved February 3, 2015 from
    http://www.amazon.com/Brian-Tracy/e/B001H6OMRI

17 Restore International. What We Do. Retrieved April 1, 2015 from
    http://restoreinternational.org/what-we-do/.

18 Goff, Bob. *Love Does: Discover a Secretly Incredible Life in an
    Ordinary World.* Nelson, Thomas, Inc. May 2012.

19 Bible Gateway, English Standard Version, Retrieved
    April 2, 2015 from https://www.biblegateway.com/
    passage/?search=Isaiah+54%3A17&version=ESV.

20 Kruse, Kevin. "Stephen Covey: 10 Quotes That Can Change Your
    Life," *Forbes,* July 16, 2012. Retrieved April 21, 2015 from http://
    www.forbes.com/sites/kevinkruse/2012/07/16/the-7-habits/

21 DeWitt, Sheryl. "Developing Friendships That Last," *Focus on the Family,* 2000. Retrieved April 21, 2015 from http://www.focusonthefamily.com/parenting/teens/developing-friendships-that-last

22 Tavros, Carol and Elliot Aronson, *Mistakes Were Made (But Not By Me),* 2007, Houghton Mifflin Harcourt, Inc.

23 Festinger, Leon, Henry Riecken, and Stanley Schachter, *When Prophecy Fails: A Social and Psychological Study of a Modern Group That Predicted the Destruction of the World.* Harper-Torchbooks, January 1, 1956.

24 Anderson, Amy Rees, "Admitting You Were Wrong Doesn't Make You Weak – It Makes You Awesome!", Forbes.com, May 1, 2013. Retrieved April 24, 2015 from http://www.forbes.com/sites/amyanderson/2013/05/01/admitting-you-were-wrong-doesnt-make-you-weak-it-makes-you-awesome/

25 Gelinas, Ryan and Krista Munroe-Chandler, "Psychological Skills for Successful Ice Hockey Goaltenders." *Athletic Insight, The Online Journal of Sport Psychology,* 2006. Retrieved April 30, 2015 from http://www.athleticinsight.com/Vol8Iss2/HockeySkills.htm

26 Lewis, C.S. *Mere Christianity.* Macmillan Publishing Company, New York, 1943.

27 Gladwell, Malcolm, *Blink: The Power of Thinking Without Thinking,* Little, Brown and Company, New York, 2007

28 Feloni, Richard. "23 Incredibly Successful People Who Failed At First," Business Insider, March 7, 2014. Retrieved May 14, 2015 from http://www.businessinsider.com/successful-people-who-failed-at-first-2014-3

29 Fry, Maddy. "Bono Biography," www.ATU2.com. Retrieved July 2, 2015 from http://www.atu2.com/band/bono/

30 Denzel Washington Biography, IMDB.com. Retrieved July 3, 2015 from http://www.imdb.com/name/nm0000243/bio